BOO iiwii

it is what it is.

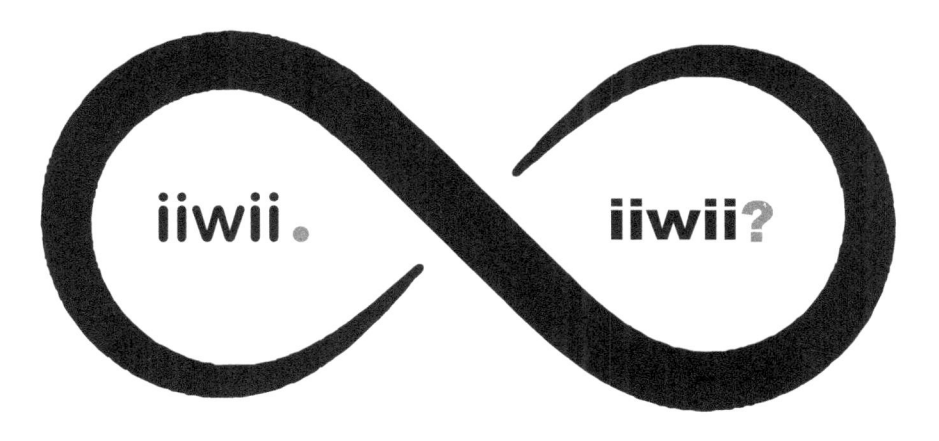

iiwii.

iiwii?

is it what it is?

KATHY LEWIS SAWYER

Published by Wheatmark®
2030 East Speedway Blvd., Suite 106
Tucson, Arizona 85719 USA
www.wheatmark.com

ISBN: 979-8-88747-176-1 (paperback)
ISBN: 979-8-88747-177-8 (hardcover)
ISBN: 979-8-88747-178-5 (ebook)
LCCN: 2024913235

Author photos on cover and page 78 of part two are by EchoStarmarker.com.

In memory of four formidables
Marjorie, Anne, JoAnne, and Georganne
and their insistence that our stories be remembered

∞

CONTENTS

→ THE FLIPPING POINT ←
(flip the book over to read part two)

INTRODUCTION

I recently read that we must write the book we most need to read. At first, I found that idea odd—almost idiotic. Aren't we supposed to write on a subject about which we, in the worst case, know at least something or, in the best case, are considered by some, even if just ourselves, to be an expert? Yet here I am, writing a book about a subject that not only eludes my mastery but also haunts me nearly every day and sometimes every hour: simple, everyday, ordinary acceptance.

It's something we've all experienced; we feel a situation should have gone one way, ideally the way we had carefully planned for it to go, and suddenly—*bam*—it doesn't.

For me, it is acceptance of the *small things*: my computer going offline at just the wrong moment, my iPad irretrievably erasing the first carefully crafted chapter of this book, and the Bermuda Triangle for socks, pens, and matches in my household.

It is also acceptance of the *not-so-small* things that I wrestle with: the heart-gripping upheaval of countries at war, untimely deaths, and catastrophic disasters plaguing the planet, from climate change and pandemics to global systemic and human burnout.

Many of us are struggling to find our way to acceptance. And yet, to make matters even worse, it is then, often midsentence as we try to express and navigate this stuff, we hear a phrase that some well-meaning bystander utters with a shrug of the shoulder. What is it they say?

"It is what it is."

These five words—equal parts highly annoying *and* aptly appropriate, depending on the situation, person, or mood of the moment—have infiltrated our daily lives and have become even more pervasive as an answer to the meaning of life than, say, "42," as espoused in *The Hitchhiker's Guide to the Galaxy* ("42" is the mysterious numerical answer to everything, according to a fictional supercomputer named "Deep Thought"). In keeping with its author Douglas Adams's short answer, I've given the phrase its own acronym: **iiwii**. I like to think it has a certain ring to it when pronounced with the long *e*, as "ee-wee."

With that in mind and a snazzy title—*Book of iiwii*—I was on a roll. Could both **it is what it is.** and what I call its opposite, **is it what it is?**, be the fodder for dealing with the inevitable tricky and tough situations that life, like a maddening game of whack-a-mole, shoves at us to figure out? If it could work for me, in a book I so badly needed to deal with all of life's frustrations, could it also help you, dear reader?

You'll have your own examples, but here are a couple of mine. When is it time to do the "bloom where we're planted" thing and simply accept a situation or life *as it is*? And when is it time to pull ourselves up, put a stake in the ground, and do something different from *what is*? How do we know *when* to do which one? How do we know *how* to do each one? Do *we* decide, or does something else decide for us?

Not unlike the annoying *it is what it is* phrase that I'd struggled to shake, these questions took on the same boomerang feel. No matter how hard I tossed them away, they would just come back and hit me in the head or smack dab in the heart. Finally, I accepted they weren't going anywhere, so I needed to embrace rather than resist them. What were these questions asking me to ponder?

At this stage, the book was a long way off, but curiosity evolved into a mild obsession. For myself, I wanted to learn the answers to these questions. Even more, I wanted to see if there might emerge some kind of formula or framework that could be applied. Could I find something that no one else had figured out? Probably unlikely, but why not try? Then, unexpectedly, more questions started coming my way. They were *not* the ones I was intently researching right then, but, I admit, they had merit.

"*Why* are you doing all this? And for whom?" my friend Shirin asked me one day after I'd given her a rough outline of some of my *Book of iiwii* thoughts and stories.

I had asked myself that same question several times. My answer, I realized, was simple and honest: *selfishness*. I wanted to do this deep dive into acceptance and its opposite for myself. I wanted to see if some of the ways we do and don't make choices around acceptance and change could shed some light on my own actions and inactions, as well as some unusual and fascinating choices made by my ancestors.

The bar was set comfortably low. I hadn't pretended to myself for a moment that I was even remotely qualified to be writing about any of this. Then, as it unfolded, I put a more substantial amount of time into this effort than I ever thought I would, and it occurred to me that I might want to make my findings available to others who might find them valuable. Maybe it *would* even turn into a book with actual pages and chapters, a title, and a cover.

Then came more questions, this time from my youngest daughter. With her throwing out a few crumbs of interest in what I was doing, I tried to explain some of the themes and insights I wanted to convey. She listened patiently and then asked, "Hmmm . . . shouldn't you have some credentials or something to present material like this?"

Bingo! I was already a step ahead on that one, with the low-bar strategy already in place. My slightly more sophisticated reply to her went something like this: "Well, I love that question. It is precisely because I am *unqualified* that I feel capable. I don't feel hobbled by certain schools of thought, teachings, or theories. I get to make up my own. I am truly writing the book I need to read, and, in a way, I have become my own test audience. If it works for me—"

"It will work for others," she finished.

Either way, whether any answers to any questions about what I was doing exactly fit, I was finding as I wrote *Book of iiwii* that it was becoming less about others' insights—my original intention—and more my own personal story. It was a space, at times like a cozy café and at other times a rollercoaster, where my right-brain desire for creative musings would meet my left-brain demand for order and structure. I am the offspring of a photographer and a neurosurgeon, so maybe this explains these two different sides that hound me constantly.

Through the act of creating and writing, I tapped into both sides and invited them to join forces. I unexpectedly became a storyteller in addition to my ever-emerging skillset of being a researcher of random tidbits and a lover of frameworks. I used personal experiences, intertwining them with threads of wisdom, theories, and insights around concepts of acceptance and questioning.

With a spirit that constantly seemed to get pulled toward asking the bigger questions, I realized I had stumbled on some unusual perspectives that may help others in the all-encompassing quest to "do life." For those of you who have figured out that quest, this is likely not the book for you. For those who grapple with finding their own yellow brick road, I encourage you to enjoy taking a break and pull up a front-row seat to see someone else's quest-in-progress.

Part one of *Book of iiwii*—**it is what it is.**—is written for anyone who is interested in understanding when and how to deal with a situation that may be very hard to accept. When do we need to see a difficult situation as the incubator for a potential pearl? What starts off as a gritty irritant that just needs to be left alone and shut away for quite a while may well transform into something unexpectedly beautiful, possibly even precious.

In part one, we experience a *call to rest* and are challenged to learn new ways of being around the themes of acceptance, stillness, and embracing mystery. These new learnings open the way to what I call *ancestral ahas*, where what has often been passed down to us as the way to "do life" is delightfully challenged with varied perspectives on actually letting things be, doing nothing, and going with the flow. This exploration will reveal some interesting and counterintuitive thinking. For example, sometimes by us quite simply *doing nothing*, a situation may, and often does, remedy itself.

Part two—**is it what it is?**—requires us, both literally and figuratively, to turn things on their head. The act of physically turning the book upside down—yes, it's printed that way on purpose—mirrors the mental shift required when we know we have to change things up and flip our current approach on its head.

Part two is about when we realize we *do* need to ask some hard questions like: When is enough enough? When do we need to view a rough situation for just what it is—hurtful, unsustainable—and recognize we have a *call to action*? Here, we are challenged to unlearn some of our old, possibly outdated, ways of being around themes of questioning, doing, and building something new.

This process of unlearning, which I have *learned* the hard way, has cleared some space for that ancestral healing to begin, which is discussed at the end of part two. When can we no longer accept the status quo that our family members often clung to like barnacles on an old barge? What do we need to do to step out of our silky-smooth comfort zones and create some ripples in our own little pond or elsewhere?

To respond to these questions, we must explore some unusual terrain and, from both sides, experience the *Book of iiwii* as a journey of envisioning—to either accept or deny situations—wrapped up in both unconventional *and* conventional wisdom. To help you deal with your own demons, I invite you to read on and let **iiwii** guide you to greater harmony for facing what must be accepted and fighting that which should not. Are you ready to begin?

PART ONE

it is what it is.

iiwii → *pronounced: /ēwē/*

iiwii.

CONTENTS

→ THE FLIPPING POINT ←
(flip the book over to read part two)

1

The Origin Story I

A story told is a life lived.
—Diana Gabaldon
(American author and scientist, PhD in quantitative behavior ecology)

I will begin at the earliest moment I can remember—the one in which this whole ridiculous yet life-altering journey started. I was at my doctor's office, agitated when what should have been a twenty-minute appointment ended up being about two hours. As I was writing my copay check—*check*: an instrument of financial payment from the prehistoric years, which, by the way, I still sometimes use today—I looked down and saw them: the fateful words that became the starting point of what was to become my **iiwii** journey.

They comprised a quote, unobtrusively taped onto the counter—yellowed, tattered, and missed by the masses, I'm sure, but picked up by me due to my extreme frustration and need to distract my thoughts somewhere. I've always really liked quotes, and sometimes they even nudge me out of a cloudy mood. My mood was verging on downpour right then.

Penned by Rainer Maria Rilke, the quote simply said, "Let life happen to you. Believe me: life is in the right, always."

As I ripped out the completed check—demonstrating a touch of mild passive-aggressive behavior—I thought, "You have got to be kidding me. Life is in the right—*always*? Who is this Rainer Maria gal, and what the heck rock does she live under? Let life happen to you? Just roll over like a spineless echidna, and let yourself be walked on like a doormat, one who has been held captive in a doctor's office for the afternoon?" My inner response to this ridiculous piece of non-wisdom boiled down to *"Believe me: life is NOT in the right almost always!"*

But wait; there's more. Why is it, when you finally see a quote written by a woman, it is idiotic and makes no sense? Have you ever noticed how many of the quotes you read have been penned by men? Similarly with cartoons in the Sunday paper, but that's going down another rant route that I don't need to address now. But I'm glad I mentioned it; check it out some Sunday.

OK, so by now, if you are an astute reader and up on your quotees—or is it *quoters*?—you will know that Rainer Maria Rilke is a man, not a woman. Actually, he was apparently a hugely acclaimed poet and womanizer. If you do a quick Google search on him, you will find he lived a multifaceted bohemian life before bohemians were invented. His perspective of "go with the flow . . . life is in the right, *always*"[1] was a convenient umbrella philosophy, as it turns out, under which to live his unconventional life in the late 1800s.

Maybe it was my general irritation at the irksome wrenches that had been thrown into my afternoon that day, but, whatever the cause, I could not get that quote out of my mind.

As often happens, at least in my world, once I open the door to one particular, and often new, concept, it's as though a magnet starts to pull other similar concepts out of the ether and onto my path.

The reason I had been at the doctor's office that day was because I was nursing a massive sinus infection and had a trip planned the following weekend to see two of our kids who were away at college. Fortunately, life *did* turn out to be "in the right," and my visit to the doctor got me the prescription I needed to clear my sinuses and head out of town.

And this is when my odd, decade-long journey took its next step. En route to the Raleigh-Durham airport, I had a layover in Las Vegas. Below is an excerpt I wrote in a notebook at the time:

I heard the phrase at the airport just a couple days ago. A man used it while trying to wrap up a conversation on his cell phone so he could get in line. I seem to hear it everywhere now that I am listening for it; it was even the parting comment (as I'd read in the news while trying to drown out the sounds of slot machines) that our ruffled state governor apparently gave to the president in a huff before turning abruptly around on the tarmac to leave him. "It is what it is." You read about it, mumble it to yourself, and often say it with a shrug of exasperated shoulders when you are just done putting up with something anymore.

Is it a form of abdication or perhaps people resigning themselves to a set of circumstances they know are beyond their capacity to change? Does it have a negative connotation? Quite often, it does.

It was at this point that I became obsessed with this phrase, or, better said, it became obsessed with me. I could not get it out of my head. Because I like to create acronyms, while driving one day a few weeks after this trip, I started playing around and realized the acronym for *it is what it is* was IIWII. Ee-wee. And then I thought about the game Wii, which our kids at the time were obsessed with, and decided I liked the look of all lowercase letters—**iiwii**. A bit of an homage as well to one of my favorite poets, e. e. cummings.

And so **iiwii** was born. Admittedly, I was not the first to come up with this acronym. After I first googled it about a decade ago, there was one reference I found. It was for the IIWII Tee Shirt Shop somewhere down in Florida. Today, there are over 350,000 references to the phrase.

That said, for me at that time it did feel like birthing a fun, new expression of this slightly obtuse phrase. On reflection, better than *birthing* is perhaps *germinating*. My **iiwii** understanding was a long way yet to fruition. Its gestation period had just begun. The core idea floating around in my womb-like creative abyss was the Rilke quote about "life is in the right, always." Somehow, when that idea intersected with *it is what it is*, a new creation began, and it just continued to grow.

The kernel of this idea was that if, through the far stretches of my imagination, Rilke's comment was correct, then maybe this growing, and slightly obnoxious, phrase **iiwii** was our new cultural equivalent of *whatever, WTF, whatevs, What can I do about it anyway?* It addressed something unsolvable, unknown, or too hard to figure out. Curiously, it was an outlook and attitude that seemed to be diametrically opposed to what I had always believed we were supposed to have.

The following were my next thoughts, which supported this idea, circa 2009, found in that same lofty spiral notebook:

We are a nation, I keep reading, of human "doings," not "beings." When a situation is not to our liking, we have been coached, encouraged, and rewarded since youth to question the assumptions and challenge ourselves—only to accept, or at least strive for, the very best in all that we do. The entire cultural, moral, and intellectual wiring of our nation was based on this. All the early discoveries pointed to this outlook as the fundamental driver behind the development and refinement of our national existence and well-being.

What if, with the turning of the page into the twenty-first century, a paradigm shift is starting to happen? Are the outlooks, tools, and philosophies that got us this far as a collective melting pot of American humanity perhaps outdated? The more we push, assert, and try to drive our points home and our policies onto others, the more this approach seems archaic and oddly masterful at achieving almost the exact opposite of what we want.

As a sidenote, I was a foreign affairs and Russian history major in college with an international business MBA as the cherry on top of my educational layer cake. Thus, my journal entries admittedly can seem somewhat different.

So if the rise of **iiwii** was indeed starting to become an indicator of a new concept, a window into a new cultural attitude of "whatever"—and certainly starting to be heard more often—I wondered where and when this phrase originated. So I did some research. Here is what I found.

ORIGINS OF AN ORDINARY PHRASE

It is what it is. Often overused, notably vague, and maddeningly obnoxious at times, this phrase has found its way into the English lexicon over the last decade. Its use has multiplied, being an especially useful utterance, it seems, for media-limelight groups like politicians, athletes, coaches, and movie stars. What does this phrase mean, and what are its origins? Some background may be helpful in understanding the concept of **iiwii.**

In 2006, columnist William Safire was intrigued enough by this phrase that he devoted a worthy article to its description: "It Is What It Is: Using Tautophrases to Duck and Deflect." He claims, "The phrase, racing through the language, shows no sign of tiring." He traces it back to a Nebraskan journalist in 1949 who was writing about the ruggedness of the land and its influence on creating strength of character for the early pioneers. Safire quotes J. E. Lawrence, who wrote in the *Nebraska Journal,* "[This] new land is harsh, and vigorous, and sturdy. It scorns evidence of weakness. There is nothing of shame or hypocrisy in it. It is what it is, without apology."[2]

Safire informs us that this expression is a "tautophrase," with *tauto* meaning "the same." Its uses can be purposefully vague: "It all depends on what the meaning of It is what it is is." It can also be a useful sort of a brush-off, as he observes, "Often accompanied by a shrug, it is used to deflect inquiry with panache."[3]

Politicians have picked up this phrase with fervor, using it to replace the outworn phrase "no comment" made popular, Safire comments, by Winston Churchill in 1946. It was used by George W. Bush, Bill Clinton, and several other politicians on more than one occasion. Similarly, athletes have been quoted using this expression many times over the last several years as a conveniently vague go-to phrase that is ingeniously multipurpose. Somehow it seems to say more than "no comment," and yet no one is sure exactly what it means.

My research continued on the origins of what was becoming to me an increasingly more multifaceted phrase. I say "research" loosely; we were just hitting the era where the mere typing of a question into an internet browser yielded more than one could ever find in weeks of the now-archaic type of library research I used in my younger years. This ability to find instantaneous information on every conceivable topic, in and of itself, became part of the fun of my **iiwii** exploration.

The next nugget I found was an article written on February 15, 2008, by *Columbia Journalism Review* columnist Douglas McCollam. Since February 15 is also my birthday, I thought there was extra synchronicity in this find. McCollam goes further back to trace the roots of the phrase *it is what it is*.[4]

He acknowledges Safire's article and the Nebraska reference but then digs deeper and finds a reference to the phrase from a much earlier source. John Locke, the fifteenth-century philosopher, penned a piece entitled "An Essay Concerning Human Understanding," in which he states that "essence may be taken for the very being of anything, whereby it is what it is." This seems a bit cryptic, but if you read it a couple of times, it sort of makes sense.

Contributors to the online Urban Dictionary of Phrases postulate that a version of the phrase, if stretched, could go back as far as biblical times, when Pontius Pilate is supposed to have said in John 19:22, "What I have written I have written," only to be topped by the God of Exodus claiming, "I am that I am" (Ex. 3:14).

OK, since we're on a roll, why not just exhaust this topic and do one final, full sweep?

Popular definitions referenced online, these from more of the Urban Dictionary contributors, ranged from a "kind of Zen-ish generic response" to "a simple reply to an obvious statement of fact of which there is little or nothing that can be done to change the situation or action."[5]

In my own experience, I have found the phrase *it is what it is* can mean many things and be used in several ways:

- tastefully dismissive ("deflecting inquiry with panache")
- frustratingly resigned to a situation that appears to have no solution
- elegantly extricating ourselves from a topic of conversation that has hit a wall
- a crisp excuse to make a hasty exit (like the man on the phone in the airport)
- a cover-up or a way to divert attention
- a cop-out
- a handy excuse *not* to change, even seen as "dangerous" by some
- an abdication of responsibility, shutting down creative problem-solving and conceding defeat
- a pointer, according to some recent enlightened thinkers, toward transformative acceptance

McCollam concludes that "there is great power in those five little syllables." It is "an amazingly flexible" phrase.[6] Mr. McCollam, I agree. Its versatility is endless.

TAKING OVER MY LIFE

Whichever it was, catchall cliché or piece of enlightened brilliance, ridiculously overused or holding infinite possibility in its vagueness, *it is what it is* was starting to drive me nuts. I was hearing it everywhere and, even more agonizingly, finding myself repeating it all the time too. Once I made the leap from *it is what it is* to **iiwii**, the phrase at least became more entertaining. It was a fun, glide-off-the-tongue word: **iiwii . . . iiwii . . . iiwii.**

It also started to grow in significance. It was not just an acronym. For me, it was a word that, for reasons unknown at that point, gradually started to take on a whole new shift in meaning from its phrase of origin.

I decided to add a period after it for emphasis—**iiwii.**—which made it a complete concept all in one acronymic word. I even gave it its own font so it could stand out when I was typing it: **iiwii.**

This shortened version reflected something different to me: not the idea of **it is what it is**—so what, dismiss it, disregard, and move on—or **it is what it is**—I'm settling, giving up, throwing in the towel. Somehow **iiwii** seemed to detach from all those meanings and elevate to a different status: **iiwii.** Could it be a vehicle for acceptance? A pathway to embracing flow? A back route to flourishing? A methodology for embracing the unembraceable? A ticket to transformation?

Strangely, all these ideas started jumbling together like very rough stones in a rock polisher, tumbling around for weeks, months, and then years—becoming more and more polished—until, at long last, they were finally begging to be released, rinsed off, and shared with whoever might be interested.

And so, "**iiwii.**"—the lowercase, declarative word-sentence, palindromic acronym to a tautophrase with a period after it—was born.

FIRESIDE CHAT

The problem then surfaced: Where do I even begin? In some ways, this is a huge topic, and in other ways, it seems very narrow. Seriously, I wondered, who would want to read this?

Then I decided to take a huge leap and share my secret—that I might try to write this book—with someone I knew would not ask me hard questions or kill my dream. The recipient of my I'm-thinking-about-writing-a-book-like-everyone-else-in-the-world secret was none other than my oldest daughter, Kristen.

The big reveal happened this way. We were lodged in a lodge on a chilly weekend when she had joined my husband and me on a trek upstate. It was the lovely El Tovar Lodge right at the edge of the Grand Canyon. He was hiking down, and we were staying topside, so the timing was perfect. It was a rugged high sixties / low seventies outside, perfect weather for snuggling in big comfy chairs in front of a massive fireplace; we live in southern Arizona, so anything in the sixties is easily considered "fireplace weather."

It was in this cozy mother-daughter moment that I shared my idea with her. I was even so bold as to share my outline and some of my notes.

"Hmmm . . . so how will you stretch this topic out long enough to make a book that isn't incredibly dry and boring—and possibly *preachy*?" I'm not sure those were her exact words, but somehow that's how whatever she said got translated by the negative mind-lingo app lodged in my head.

Immediately, I thought, *Bad idea. I'm never ever going to mention this idea to anyone else. More hard questions. Dream killed.*

I looked down at the lovely, jewel-toned, ruby-red carpet, bespeckled with charred cinders of my self-esteem, along with a few ashes from the roaring fire, and said, "Hmmm . . . well, I hadn't really thought that it would be boring and preachy, but I appreciate your input." This was all through a noticeable grimace, revealing a very feeble attempt to do a mom-modeling-resiliency thing.

Kristen, a wise twentysomething millennial, saw right through it. "You're sad that I said that, aren't you? You have some really great ideas. Do you want some of my thoughts on how to make it interesting?"

"Hmmm . . . I guess so," I half-heartedly replied. "Wow," I thought, "if I can't even take honest observations and a suggestion or two from Kristen, how am I ever going to do this writing thing?"

Then, with a spark of perspective, she encouragingly said, "In one of your notes, you referred to a story that you wanted to share to illustrate the point, right?"

I replied, with an odd sort of role-reversal sensation, "Uh-huh."

"And you love using quotes and also having something be practical, right?"

This time a nod was all I could muster. I had already decided to ditch the idea. There are too many books out there anyway.

"So why don't you create sort of a framework where you start with a story to explain your concept for that chapter and slap a quote at the top of the chapter like everyone else seems to do? But your quotes won't be like anyone else's, Mom. They'll be way more original."

She was trying to butter me up. It was very transparent, but it was slightly working. I also love the idea of frameworks.

"I'm listening," I said, in a slightly disengaged, shrug-of-the-shoulder way while peering into the fire like people do when they want to leave a conversation but don't want to be rude. I think that's called *defecting in place*. Anyway, I actually was listening at this point, even though my eyes were averted.

"And then you could maybe add some kind of a practice tool at the end of each chapter that helps reinforce learning that concept."

Did I mention she was a sixth-grade teacher at that time? She was starting to lose me again. Tools? Who am I to give anyone tools anyway? Or wisdom? Remember, this was the book I needed to *read*, not write!

And then, in a stroke of brilliance, she said, "We've got all afternoon, Mama. Why don't you tell me some stories? What was that one you referenced in your notes? Something about a cave?"

And so it began.

2

Acceptance

What would come, would come . . . and you
would have to meet it when it did.
—J. K. Rowling
(British author and philanthropist)

Colossal Scare at Colossal Cave

I am holding our two-year-old son, Bennett—more like clutching him with all my might—while walking next to his big sister, Kristen, a whopping three years old, as we follow my husband's brother into a black pit of terror. The walls are wet. The smell is earthy, musty, and chalky. Something is dripping on our heads. Shouldn't people know that taking children who are two and three years old into a dark cave with a noticeably narrow walkway and only a flimsy rail separating onlookers from a huge black abyss is *not* a good idea?

On this particular occasion, it is just me with the two kids, which typically would not be a big deal at all. With my brother-in-law, a geologist, already long out of sight, no doubt salivating over the stalactites up ahead, I know something is not right. The problem is that I am starting to experience waves of claustrophobia. So what do I do? Instead of fight or flight, I do a freeze and squeeze, holding Bennett so tightly he then joins me in my mini–panic attack, naturally making him struggle and cry, wanting to flee from my arms.

As he is flailing about, I realize that if I put him down to walk, he is shorter than the railing. So falling into the black pit would, of course, most certainly happen. You might be asking, "Why not put him down and just hold his little hand, so he doesn't fall into the black abyss, and get a move on?" Well, when I get nervous or drink too much coffee, my hands get sweaty. Not just moist but slippery-slide wet, and in this instance, they were dripping as much as the rock formations over my head.

Thoughts coursed through my overstimulated brain: *I shouldn't have listened to my brother-in-law* ("The kids will love this supercool place called Colossal Cave"). *My husband should be here with me. I should be calmer, stronger. I shouldn't have had two kids so close together in age. I shouldn't have ever thought going into a cave was a good idea.* And so the pile of shoulds and shouldn'ts grew and grew. That's when it really hit me: *we are all alone; we can hardly even see anything above us or, for that matter, much in front of us either.* And I froze.

Whether it was for a moment or an hour, I couldn't say, but thankfully some sort of survival instinct kicked in, or maybe it was just my son kicking me in the side. Either way, it worked. In a valiant attempt to shake myself out of this frozen stupor, settle down, and divert attention from the swirl of shoulds, it came to me to do the exact opposite of what I wanted to do. I paused.

Somewhere deep inside, something said, "Be OK with just standing still for a moment, even though every fiber of your being wants to run out of this dark tunnel like a screaming banshee clutching her young." Taking a moment to stop and pause, as hard as that was, at least was doable, as I noticed there were no other cave visitors with us. This should have been my first sign of why we should not have been in this cave. But there goes more shoulding. See how easy it is?

I then take a deep breath and somehow find the wherewithal to call forth sleuth number-one skill of child-raising: redirection. With an index finger dramatically pointing upward at those "amazing icicle stalag-whatever formations" over our heads, I started to settle down, look around, and notice some quasi-interesting things. As I settled, the kids settled too. It didn't seem so dark, and the formations all around us actually started to feel a bit more inviting than terrifying. I realized I needed to try to make the best of the situation exactly as it was. I took a long exhale and then breathed in "cave experience."

My **iiwii.** moment had arrived. I moved past all the resentful shoulds, shoved myself back into the reality of the situation, and simply accepted it. *Nobody is going to rescue me. Nobody is going to tell me exactly how to do what I know I need to do, which is to calm down, embrace the drips coming down on our heads, and successfully get us out of here!*

So yes, we did ultimately make it out of Colossal Cave, which was one big, colossal, claustrophobic cluster. I did the equivalent of a Hail Mary run, unfroze myself, commented on some of the rock formations, and told the kids that we had to find Uncle David "*right away* to see if he found the big one!" Big what? Who knows? I make it up as I go along, but it did the trick: captured their attention for the moment, and got us moving forward. We managed somehow to make it all the way through and around the large loop that then brought us back out of the cave. As I literally and figuratively saw the light at the end of this damp, dank, creepy, looping tunnel overlooking the abyss of no return, I could finally breathe. We were out.

Kristen, thankfully tall for her robust age of three, had not been in jeopardy of falling into the pit and had merrily skipped after Uncle Rockhound, as we lovingly called him, asking him about the "stalagmites Mommy showed us back there." I overheard this as Bennett and I exited the cave after them and thought, "Wow, I have no memory of saying anything back there." I was kind of ready to pat myself on the back until I heard Unc replying, "Well, that is wrong. Those were actually stalactites hanging from the top of the cave. Stalagmites come up from the bottom." Ugh and eye roll. Not even a crumb of kudos after this harrowing ordeal.

As for me, once out of the cave of doom, I slowly let loose the vice grip I had on Bennett, who had sort of grafted into my left hip and ribcage by this point. I pried my pruned fingertips off him, no doubt leaving permanent handprint indentations on his miniature little-boy back. Hmmm . . . I wonder if they are still there. He is now in his thirties.

No Shoulding

DON'T SHOULD ON YOURSELF

How often do we should on ourselves? How often do we should on others? How often do we stand in a big, smelly pile of should and find we are unable to take a step out of it? It is amazing to consider what runs through our minds in a moment of panic. The feelings seem to crystallize into the mental version of a dripping, musty stalag-whatever that hangs in the shadowy interior of our brain: an ever-present reminder, warning us, for example, never to go into a dark cave with inadequate rails next to a pitch-black abyss.

The first **iiwii.** theme is all about the mastery of acceptance. By accepting reality—whatever it is that is right in front of us—we start to change the inclination to should on others and ourselves. Inappropriate shoulding can become habit forming. We begin to break this habit, which is a messy and undesirable prospect by anyone's standards, as we embark on the path of **iiwii.** Accept it. Period.

Simple, right?

Hardly. And did I actually use the word *mastery* in the last paragraph? I have been working on this idea of acceptance since the Colossal Cave incident, at least, and am still far, far away from mastering anything resembling it. As mentioned, that's about thirty years and counting. We write the book we most need to read.

I have to say, it is not for lack of trying to read books about this topic and many others that I still ended up feeling the pull to write about my own **iiwii.** journey. In the last three decades, I have piled up dozens of self-help books, stuffing them on various shelves, in closets, and in boxes around the house. Somehow, if I could find just the right theory, framework, pearl of wisdom, or morsel of enlightenment, then I might be able to crack the code on this acceptance stuff—and everything else in life I didn't understand.

Embrace the Zig Zag

WHAT WE RESIST PERSISTS

As I have embarked on this quest, as with most other initiatives, I am drawn toward simple questions like: How do we get from point A to point B? My preference always is the straight line and preferably a simple 1-2-3 formula. The reality is that straight lines to anything rarely exist. For me, it's a zigzaggy, circuitous experience most of the time. I somehow always have to go down to go up and then have to go up to go down, with a bit of sideways and upside down thrown in.

And so, while I continued in my quest for a straightforward approach, I realized ditching the resistance, even to zigzags and detours, was a part of it all. I continued to try to understand how we shift from shoulding to acceptance, with my starting point A being that original quote from Rilke, the one about life being in the right, *always*. So far, it hadn't been such a good starting point. Being stuck in a cave was about as far from "life being in the right always" as I could imagine right then.

We all have our Colossal Cave moments. We suddenly find ourselves in the middle of a situation we do not know how to get out of. Enter the woulda, shoulda, couldas. But where do they lead? To acceptance? Absolutely not. For me, the cave shoulding led me right into the jaws of resistance. The frozen thought bubble over my head would have read something like "I cannot accept this situation as it is. There is, simply put, *no* way. No way out, no way back, no way forward. We are trapped. I think there is a good chance we are going to fall into the abyss and be done."

That line of thinking, not shockingly, led to immobility—a freeze and squeeze, my poor little boy's back in this case. What we resist persists. We feel trapped, with no way to move. As long as I was in the clutches of resisting the moment, I was its victim. It kept getting worse. Strangely, when I did suddenly freeze, it gave me a moment to pause and, after squeezing the air out of Bennett's lungs, take a couple of breaths while still completely tethered to our little patch of cave path.

Then, in that pause, it was as though I suddenly experienced a snap-out-of-it reverberation all the way down my quivering, goosebumped legs. I snapped out of the head swirl and came back down to earth—or inside earth, as was my case. Some call it being present, or being in the now, or even present-moment awareness. I call it the **iiwii.** moment. I crossed over from resistance to acceptance.

Animals, birds, and reptiles in the wild do this all the time. We are familiar with the flight-or-fight situations, but one that gets less play and is equally, if not more, important is the freeze reaction. It is a profound form of very quick acquiescence to and instant acceptance of a situation from which they know they cannot fight or flee. I witnessed an example of this just the other day as I was in my chair reading with a large picture window in front of me.

Suddenly, I heard the telltale thud. A bird had flown right into the glass of the window and, in a fluster of feathers, took a free fall to the ground. When I dashed out to see if it was all right, it appeared to be alive and yet totally frozen in place. It was on the ground, possibly in pain, possibly just dazed and/or frozen in fear since now there was a person (me) suddenly on the scene. After flying into what looked like air and then crashing down in a split second, it went into a state of immobility, momentary shutdown.

This is the freeze response. It's as though our system goes offline and then, when the threat level is ascertained and deemed to be OK—there were no broken wings or bones for the bird—it is like a reboot happens: the body slowly or quickly comes back online, and we can get a move on.

Like the bird that suddenly had a full-body quiver and then flew off, no worse for the wear, my cave situation similarly had that same sort of feel—like a slow-motion smashing into a glass window of surprise. Like the bird, I was able to do my own version of a shudder and flap, getting my kids mobilized and doing what we needed to do to get out of that place with some moments of enjoyment as well as our dignity, family, and well-being in one piece.

This leads me to my point B (did you note the slightly zigzag way I got here?), which happens to be another **iiwii.** revelation quotation. It is a more intriguing version of the Rilke quote, in addition to coming from what turned out to be, for me, a most fascinating source.

> ***Everything in life that we really accept undergoes a change.***
> —Katherine Mansfield
> (New Zealand writer, essayist, and journalist, 1888–1923)

When I first saw and read this, it affected me in the same way Rilke's "life is in the right, always" quote had. Weirdly, it stopped me in my tracks. It seemed to be an equally compelling, if not a more useful and possibly hopeful, version of Rilke's rendition: you may as well just get past the resistance and on to a place of acceptance because it is from this place that change becomes possible.

This seems counterintuitive. Typically, it is because we feel we *cannot* accept something that we want it to change in the first place. What Mansfield implies is that acceptance begets change, not the other way around. How many times have we tried to change a situation or someone's mind when coming from a place of shoulding, cajoling, or badgering—all forms of resisting *what is*? Has it worked?

I remember a shoulding phone call I made once to my mom about my kids one summer. It was a textbook "my kids should" rant. What should they do? Summer stuff. Activities. Cool programs. What did they want to do? None of it. Nothing.

All my friends' kids and my kids' friends seemed besotted with summer day camps, tippy-toes ballet, Kindermusik, Tiny Tumblers, Arts 'n' Crafts for Miniature Artists and Crafters, etc., etc. This was the early 1990s, and helicopter parenting had launched from its pesky pad with my generation of parenting friends at the helm. I had totally fallen into the FOMO (fear of missing out) for parents trap: *Why don't they want to be the confident, adventurous trailblazers that all the other kids their ages seem to be? Why are they so clingy? Should I force them to go? We signed up, after all. They said they were interested. They should finish what they start, right? Even if they hate it, right? Even if their camp coun-selor* [yes, our oldest was (sort of) attending a day camp at her elementary school down the block] *said they were going to let the kids try a weird side dish of edible bug snacks. That could be fun, right?*

This was the particular swirl of thoughts and arguments I unloaded on my mom one early summer afternoon. My kid-shouldering was justi-fied, or so I thought. On the other end of the phone, my mom had been uncharacteristically quiet. When I finally stopped to catch my breath, she gave me her response, and it was three words: "Get. A. Life."

I almost fell out of my chair. "Wait, what? Me?" I replied, taken aback.

"Yes, you. If those kids are happy playing at home, in the backyard, in a mud pit, let them be. Let them be kids without a schedule while they're still little. You be the one to go right now and sign up for an art class or some version of your own tippy-toe tumbler thing that appeals to *you*. If you're doing things that bring you joy, that will make more of a difference in the long run than forcing them to do some inane program, especially one serving up dead bugs. They see you doing things you like to do, and eventually they will find the things they want to do, and believe me, you will not be able to stop them."

Weirdly, I think my mother could have been an undercover anarchist in another life. She certainly would have bucked the hovering-parent revolution taking place in my day. She was not a child coddler, that's for sure. Underneath the veneer of a woman who became an adult in the 1940s and 1950s with the conventionality that was thrust on her, there was a subversive human that I only saw a few hints of—much less than I wish I had.

OK, so back to her three words. They certainly had a bit of the snap-out-of-it effect. Get a life. I did it. I accepted that maybe it wasn't the kids who needed the intervention. It was me. It was them, those small humans, I was trying to change so they would either understand or be coerced into my way of thinking. "More activity equals good, normal . . . dare I say, success?" Ugh. That's uncomfortable to admit. I wanted to change them and have them doing what "everyone" else seemed to be doing, but instead it was me who needed to change and accept that a different approach might merit consideration.

The next day, I drove to Light House Beach Arts Center and signed up for a watercolor class. Three hours every Thursday evening. My husband would hang with the kids, and I could be the one to do the summer program. I loved it and took Thursday night art classes for years after that.

It's so annoying when mothers are right.

Regarding the edible dead-crickets-for-snack-time adventure at Willard Elementary's day camp, I told Kristen that if she didn't want to go, she didn't have to go, and I completely meant it. Honestly, I was a bit flipped out about her potential bug-eating adventure myself. She had the option to go or just stay home and eat a normal peanut butter and jelly sandwich, with no dead parts, which she did.

Ironically, missing that edible dead-bug day of camp became something she never forgot. She actually "scolded" me in her eldest-daughter, seven-year-old way for not "making" her go after she heard from her fellow day campers that it had been "really fun eating the bugs and crickets, and they were actually really, really good!" Humorously and ironically, she has never missed an opportunity to eat edible bugs or any other type of weird food ever since.

Katherine Mansfield, whose quote about acceptance kicked off this section, would have fully supported my mother's approach. Mansfield offers a way of getting beyond the shoulding by suggesting we do the opposite of what we would usually do. Embrace the situation, as hard as it may be, and from that place the chance for change becomes more, not less, likely. Truly, this reflects the key **iiwii.** learning yet again: what we resist persists. The more I wanted the kids to do all this random stuff, the more they resisted. When I let the situation be what it was, my paint palette and brushes in hand, the kids' attitudes gradually started to shift as well. By the next summer, it was all systems—and camps and classes—go for everybody.

When it finally came time to switch from painting to writing and, years later, this **iiwii** book was at full throttle, Mansfield's upside-down angle on acceptance was something I knew I needed to explore. I had never heard of her. And so, yet again, I did my research. I have to say I was as surprised by her background as I had been when I found out Rilke was a man, not a woman. Maybe it's just me, and maybe many know her name, but here is what I found:

> Kathleen Mansfield Murry (born October 14, 1888, and died January 9, 1923) was a New Zealand writer, essayist and journalist, widely considered one of the most influential and important authors of the modernist movement. Her works are celebrated across the world, and have been published in 25 languages.
>
> Mansfield wrote short stories and poetry under a variation of her own name, Katherine Mansfield. . . . When she was 19, she left New Zealand and settled in England, where she became a friend of D. H. Lawrence, Virginia Woolf, Lady Ottoline Morrell and others in the orbit of the Bloomsbury Group. Mansfield was diagnosed with pulmonary tuberculosis in 1917, and she died in France aged 34.[1]

One of the reasons I want to highlight Mansfield is that in doing research for this book—or having research "do me," as felt more the case—it was startling how many of the quotations, books, and references were always by men. I know I mentioned this before, but it bears repeating. Don't get me wrong: I love our men, and yet, as mentioned earlier, it is amazing how, historically, many women and their creative work are still not widely known. As J. K. Rowling so aptly states in her quote at the beginning of this chapter, "What would come, would come . . . and you would have to meet it when it did." So I am "meeting" and noting this reality and accepting that it needs to change.

Katherine Mansfield exemplified the concept of *change through acceptance* in her ability to embrace a huge amount of debris that life had thrown her way—a favorite brother killed in World War I, several lovers and heartbreaks, a miscarriage of her only child, and at several points having been shunned or put down by fellow artists. And yet she elevated her spirit and accepted what "would come," allowing the heartache and resentment to become fodder for her writing.

In addition to being surprised that I'd never heard of her, there was something else that caught my attention and excitement in Mansfield's minibiography. It was the reference to the Bloomsbury Group.

As many disparate threads seem to tie, loop, and weave together in totally unexpected ways in this book—including, as an aside, the fact that the Harry Potter series was published by Bloomsbury Publishing House—the Bloomsbury Group coexisted in an early version of a 1960s commune, using as their central hub a lovely country home called Charleston, nestled in the famous downs of Sussex, south of London.

Also called the Bloomsbury Set, they were a collective of early twentieth-century English writers, intellectuals, philosophers, and artists. Included in the large group were famous names like Virginia Woolf, John Maynard Keynes, and E. M. Forster. They started out living, working, or studying together near Bloomsbury, London. Later, they migrated to the countryside.

In either location, as it turns out, Katherine was at best on the fringes of these artists. Her caustic wit and general demeanor apparently turned many of the Bloomsbury Group off, thus the shunning, which created even more of a desire to fit in. While at best their friendship was "uneasy," Virginia Woolf once wrote of Mansfield, "I was jealous of her writing—the only writing I have ever been jealous of."[2]

Tying this all back to our point B, the revelatory allure for me was both the simplicity and complexity in Mansfield's quote, which means that everything we are able to really accept in life can and eventually does undergo a change. Simple, and yet it is so hard at times to understand how this could possibly happen just by letting life do what it is going to do and focusing on our own little corner.

Regarding the Bloomsbury Group's relevance to the concept of **iiwii.**—along with an unusual and lovely surprise connection that crops up later in *Book of iiwii*—they epitomized for me this let-it-be, defect-in-place while in your own corner sort of attitude. The group was tucked away in the privacy of Charleston, their own little creative hotbed and nook in the world. Reveling in its oasis-like offerings of exquisite gardens, ponds, and inspiring vistas, Vanessa Bell, Duncan Grant, Virginia Woolf, and the others harnessed huge amounts of fiery creativity. The new thinking, energy, and expressive art forms that came from this small beehive of bohemians have been both vastly influential and legendary. They defied the rules and structures of a world beset by the frenzy and flurry of war and unrest. They, like Katherine in different circles, turned convention on its head and threw out the manual, so to speak.

I Shall

Nothing important comes with instructions.

—James Richardson

(American poet, writer, and professor)

I SHALL

How do we lower the gavel and "do life" when it comes to acceptance? How do we embrace the resistance that is wired into our very core? When reading about Katherine's various ventures, which sadly ended way too early with her demise from tuberculosis, I ran across an interview someone had with her that randomly contained the words *I shall* in it. She was talking about something regarding her intentions as a writer, but the words *I shall* were what jumped right off the page for me.

"I shall" is like saying "I will" but with much more grit. It is a word that has almost gone out of our vocabulary, and yet, when thinking about **it is what it is** (period), I think it can be beautifully repurposed for **iiwii.** It is a declaration of intent, which is what this quest is all about.

Additionally, as part of this quest, I am finding, with every year I age, there needs to be more instruction manuals. I need them to answer so many tiny little questions like, *How do we do life?* Or, more eloquently, how do we get ourselves out of the forest of resistance and into the lush meadow of acceptance? And so, as we continue on this pondering journey to discover, understand, and possibly even embrace acceptance, I shall create my own declaration of intent by providing some rest stops. To me, there are few better places to pause for some quick insight into acceptance than Eckhart Tolle, globally acclaimed author of *The Power of Now*. He writes:

Accept—then act. Whatever the present moment contains, accept it as if you had chosen it. Always work with it, not against it. Make it your friend and ally, not your enemy. This will miraculously transform your whole life.

Performing an action in the state of acceptance means you are at peace while you do it. That peace is a subtle energy vibration which then flows into what you do. On the surface, acceptance looks like a passive state, but in reality, it is active and creative because it brings something entirely new into this world.

It all revolves around some version of the same thing: "But first, accept the situation." They all make it sound so easy. Why is it easy to accept a situation when we feel, to our core, that we should have done something differently or a situation or a person should be different? This seems subtle, but it's not. It is the water we swim in so often that we're not even aware.

In another, equally brilliant book of our times titled *Loving What Is*, Byron Katie contends, "Every story is a variation on a single theme: 'This shouldn't be happening. I shouldn't have to experience this. God is unjust. Life isn't fair.'"

She nails it. Just like my cave story, the pile-on of nonacceptance shoulding started first with the situation (why the cave?) then on to those "responsible" (why did I listen to him?). Next, if left to its own devices, the shoulding can escalate toward the totally irrational (What is wrong with me that I agreed to this? Landed in a cave? Had kids? Drank coffee? etc.). The shoulds multiply at a rapid pace, making dings all over our psyches just like a mental pinball machine.

So why do we do it? Why do we continually berate ourselves for all the things we should have done but didn't do or the things we shouldn't have done but went ahead and did anyway? Beating ourselves up can actually become a life strategy. It has roots that extend way back. Remember the albino man in *The Da Vinci Code*? Remember the leg-cinching spiked dog collar (a.k.a. *cilice*) hidden under his robe? Yes, it appeared excruciatingly painful and utterly ridiculous. Too many of us have chosen some version of such mortification for thousands of years.

Now, when embroiled in one of these anciently inspired shoulding mindsets, it is exactly the time I try to call forth the *I shall* declaration and use it as a potent counterpoint to this unproductive, slightly demented yet pervasive shoulding strategy.

Moving into the *I shall* frame of mind starts us shifting into the **iiwii.** moment—that moment to refresh, when we move out of resistance into accepting *what is*. It's not the need to condone or endorse a situation; it's finding the space to say yes to what is and not fighting it. It's letting it be, at least for now. This action of *I shall* acceptance often becomes the catalyst for circumstances to shift in unexpected ways.

Stripes & Spots

STRIPES AND SPOTS

One of the biggest *I shall* intentions that often supports this positive shift in circumstances is quite simply our beliefs around the notion of trying. For example, how often do we react in a negative or positive way when we hear someone say the words "I was *trying* to do my best"?

I have noticed that this phrase, not unlike *it is what it is*, can elicit lots of different reactions. How many times have we quietly shaken our head when someone says, "Well, I *tried* to do my best," and their try-hard best not only missed the mark in our thinking but also missed the target entirely? "Why can't people just do what they're supposed to do?" we quietly mumble to ourselves. "Why can't they be more perfect? Or at least less imperfect?" With **iiwii.**, we are going from our starting point of life "always" being in the right to then—whether we think they are totally "right" or not—accepting situations as they are. In this, accepting others' attempts and efforts becomes part of it.

And it is harder than it seems. I used to be on the skeptical side of the "I'm doing my best" comment. And yet, as I've gotten older, I have shifted my thinking. Even if someone underperforms, misses the bull's eye, or blatantly walks away from something they've been asked to do, in that moment, I try(!) to encourage myself to consider that maybe they actually *were* trying to do their best. While obviously there are exceptions, I find more and more that, some days, our best is awful, even nonexistent, but it is all we can muster up. It is on days like these that I encourage myself to conjure up a favorite phrase I learned years ago, which should be its own mantra: *My friend is not perfect, nor am I, and so we suit each other admirably.*

There are times we have to accept that something is hardwired to be what we think of as "imperfect" and may not change. **it is what it is.** Otherwise, it's like looking at a tiger and hoping and praying with all our might that its stripes will change to something else like leopard spots, which we perhaps happen to like a bit better. It is just not going to happen. We either learn to see the beauty of stripes, or we don't. We work with the stripes and come to love, like, or at least understand them, or we go find a leopard. Either way, the stripes in this case remain—and always will.

I often wonder how other cultures deal with the stripes-and-spots issue, not to mention pervasive perfectionism, inner shoulding, and persistent resistance. What would a sage monk from an ashram in India do, for example, if he was stuck in a claustrophobic cave with two tiny humans in panic mode and slime dripping down on top of him while he's staring into a black-void deathtrap? All by himself?

Would he chant? Pray? Pick up his robe and run? This leads to my final question around the theme of acceptance: How *do* different parts of the world address this, and is there something that can possibly be learned from such wisdom?

Wabi-Sabi

WABI-SABI

I have been familiar for some time with the Japanese notion of *kintsugi*, which, in my understanding, celebrates the inevitable breakages, cracks, and rough spots of life with the symbolism of using gold in place of, for example,

Gorilla Glue to readhere broken pieces of pottery together. The belief is that the true gold of life lies in the places where we are most vulnerable.

I fell in love with this concept and had originally wanted to highlight it in this chapter—that is, until I learned recently of another Japanese concept that bumped kintsugi down the ladder a bit. It's called *wabi-sabi*.[3] As the simple fading-brushstroke image above implies, wabi-sabi is all about the art of noticing subtleties. As both kintsugi and wabi-sabi illustrate, all cultures deal with their own version of **iiwii**. questions focusing on acceptance and change in their own unique ways. I learned about wabi-sabi a couple years ago. This happened while co-facilitating a monthly program with humans and horses at an amazing local organization called Equinimity,[4] a Tucson-based nonprofit supporting individuals and groups who interact with a herd of six horses and a team of professionals specializing in a range of trauma-informed offerings. Our discussions would go in all sorts of directions, often before "mindfully grooming" the herd. This specific program was called Just Horsing Around (JHA), and I adored this particular group, which consisted primarily of women who had (or once had) loved ones with dementia and/or Alzheimer's disease. These courageous souls, with poise and courage, navigated the tricky waters of caretaking people they loved with all their hearts—people who no longer knew who they were. During these sessions, we would hang out with the horses—the ultimate healers on this planet, possibly along with dogs—and with each other, discussing everything under the sun, like wabi-sabi.

A way I would often describe this rejuvenating work with humans and horses is not as an intellectual understanding but more of a feeling, an experiential discovery. Wabi-sabi seems to fit into a similar category. After hearing the term in our JHA conversation, I decided (naturally) to do some research. The understanding for me that emerged was that wabi-sabi is a way of experiencing the world, often through interactions with nature or objects from nature, and noticing our sensations as we do so. Beauty and harmony emerge quietly as connections are noticed and made. We stand in the middle of the quiet and let stillness find us.

Wabi, the first concept, embraces a notion of imperfect beauty. It is the simplicity and mystery all made manifest in something as commonplace as noticing the lovely limb of a tree. We might run our hands, for example, over the rough bark of a mesquite tree, if one lives in the Sonoran Desert, and notice that it is more ticklish than coarse and scratchy, as we might have expected it to be.

Or it could be feeling the smooth, silky-soft, whiskery muzzle of a horse that decides to welcome us into its space through a barely perceptible gentle touch to our arm. This subtle gesture, which, if one is not both aware *and* present, would likely go unnoticed, and yet it is an overt display of acceptance in the language of horse. Feeling the connection that happens when one of these majestic creatures weighing half a ton and with swift-kicking reflexes decides we are safe and worthy of its trust can be a transcendent experience for many. It surpasses all the resistant shoulding we could ever muster and allows us to connect to a similar space of trust and worthiness inside ourselves.

It is my understanding that this interconnected way of being is an example of wabi's essence. It is the art of becoming still and noticing what is in front of us. It is witnessing profound beauty in a gesture or an object that evokes a heart-reverberating sensation and yet is humble in its simplicity.

Sabi, as its own concept before it links with wabi, is more about the dimension of time and its fleeting nature, honoring versus resisting the notion that all things age. Sabi celebrates wrinkles and the beauty of all the experiences that created them. It celebrates the perfection of imperfection.

There apparently is a style of Japanese textile art that evolved over hundreds of years that beautifully exemplifies wabi-sabi. My friend Li-Lin mentioned it to me one day just after I shared with her my exciting discovery of this ancient/new concept. The style is called *boro*[5] from the Japanese word *boroboro,* meaning "something tattered, reused, and repaired." She explained that it was started among those living in rural Japan as a way of patching together old and tattered pieces of fabric to extend the life of their clothing. While at one time these garments and especially the coats, now called boro jackets, were considered shameful and a sign of impoverishment, they have become in recent years exalted as a high form of textile art and, ironically, very expensive to purchase. They are meant to illustrate the exquisite beauty in simplicity, in celebrating, and in using, versus disdaining and discarding, what many consider worn, old, or outdated. This textile art seems to symbolize the passage of time and the beauty in celebrating all of the perfectly imperfect, patched-together moments that make up one's life.

As I was researching wabi-sabi, there was one other concept from Japanese culture that a few sources referenced and I found intriguingly applicable. It summarizes beautifully the **iiwii**. part-one message. Called *uketamo*, or more correctly written/pronounced "uketamow,"[6] it means "accept everything as it is" or "accept all the things naturally." The phrase apparently originated in the Dewa Sanzan mountain region of Japan, a renowned and ancient pilgrimage destination for the Yamabushi monks.[7] Translated further, one source describes its meaning as "I humbly accept with an open heart" or "acceptance to the very core."[8]

It does not mean to tolerate or in any way accept harm but rather to accept our *everyday situations* in a spirit of understanding how we can push forward, possibly see a lesson, and grow from them. In applying uketamo(w) to our growing definition of acceptance, I came up with the following examples, which may or may not have come from firsthand experiences:

- Your puppy just chewed up a Sharpie pen on your sandstone-colored (a.k.a. pristine cream) carpet.

- Your bike just detached from its rack and is bouncing down the highway behind your car.

- You spill coffee all over your clean white shirt moments before a job interview.

To each of these, if we were in the Shounai District of Yamagata, the reply might simply be "uketamo(w)." If we let ourselves get unduly upset, we will continue to compound our suffering; less reaction equals more, a quicker chance for resolution. We may as well accept it, do what we can do, and move on.

In a way, then, we could say **iiwii**. is a Western version of a wabi-sabi uketamo(w). It's a little easier to remember and certainly easier to spell, so, if for no other reasons than those, we'll continue to go with it.

To summarize, the shift to acceptance happens when we can encourage ourselves to pause, thaw the freeze, and snap out of resistance by focusing even for a moment on something else like overhead stalactites, clouds, trees, or an overhead light fixture (if you're lucky enough not to be in a cave). The power and magic of the **iiwii**. moment is that it is a stealth shortcut, nudging us out of inner resistance and opening the door to a different way to look at a situation—a way of acceptance.

iiwii. It's not about you. Ditch the inner dictator, lighten up, and take a breath.

iiwii. It's not about others. People aren't perfect, and most are trying their best; forget about them.

iiwii. It's all about saying "I shall" let what is be what is, at least for now.

ACCEPTANCE (LET IT BE)

No Shoulding

Embrace the Zig Zag

I Shall

Stripes & Spots

Wabi-Sabi

3

Do Nothing

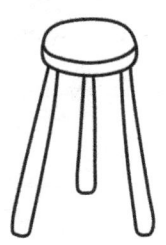

Sometimes I sits and thinks and sometimes I just sits

—Anonymous

Eye of the Storm

I am exhausted.

I am remembering back to a poster on my bedroom wall growing up that figured prominently, both on the wall and in my memory. It had a bright yellow background with one large, red, three-legged stool on it. In crooked black writing just under the three red legs were scrawled the words "sometimes I sits and thinks and sometimes I just sits." No punctuation, no attribution as to who had written those words, and no idea where I even got the poster. It has stayed with me ever since.

For me, it had a couple of connotations. It might mean, on a positive note, after we had *accepted* a certain situation and had a choice of action or not, that sometimes, if we just chose to do nothing and perhaps just sat and waited for a bit, things would simply remedy themselves.

I remember specifically, as a teen, the times I would intentionally step out of the fray of the drama of the day and go off grid for a few hours or even a day. Mind you, this was very easy to do back then, pre-internet and pre-cell-phone days. I'd reemerge, and more often than not, the drama would have completely died down, like smoldering logs that fizzle out once left alone.

I also observed a more negative connotation. It was that of doing nothing, not out of choice but more out of a feeling of being stuck. And yet even that connotation had a silver lining in that often I would find that being stuck would force me to actually take the time to stop and take stock of something that for me was very hard, both then and now: what I was feeling and/or what I had felt and what I sensed the best next step might be.

That solitary red chair and the feelings it evoked recently reemerged for me unexpectedly after decades of dormancy. I remembered it as I was writing this chapter and realized how much I loved this reemergent image. If I was a tattoo person, I'd probably tattoo it on a hidden body part.

It symbolized the exact sensation for me of finding myself being able to do absolutely nothing in a very extreme situation I experienced just a few years ago: stuck on a stool in the middle of a global tornado called COVID-19. My title was campus-wide community life director, and this exhaustion-producing, sweeping sensation of stuckness and immobility all started one day when I was at work. Here is how the "Eye of the Storm" story went down:

I had just joined our morning stand-up meeting, a highly creative invention and brilliant concept I wish I had invented. It is a meeting that by definition starts exactly at a designated time and goes exactly for a designated number of minutes—ten, in our case—with no airtime clogging, no verbal vomiting, no sitting down and getting comfortable, and no side conversations. Its sole purpose was to share only relevant news to that day, then **bam and scram;** we're done and off to do our jobs.

It was a typical Monday morning, and yet this particular meeting started with a very atypical request. Our executive director simply asked us, "Everyone, please find a chair. Grab them from the offices around and come back to my office. I need to share something with you. Last one in, close the door."

OK. Something significant was about to happen. It was the first time anyone had ever said, "Grab a chair" for a stand-up meeting. The "close the door" comment was clearly not a good sign.

"Do any of you know anyone in Kirkland, Washington?" she started.

Mumbles of no and shaking of heads ensued, paired with a hint of irritability as many members of this group were clinicians with very tight schedules, and everyone else had full departments to run, needing the usual Monday morning attention. With what was shared next, the irritability shifted to utter disbelief as an unexpected bomb was dropped: "An outbreak of the virus severe acute respiratory syndrome coronavirus 2 (SARS-CoV-2) was just reported over the weekend in a nursing home there. They are officially calling the disease COVID-19, and it does not look good. It appears to be very contagious, with three confirmed cases and one death. It looks like a significant number of the residents at this facility have been exposed, as have the caregivers and staff. At this point, there is no known cure."

Complete silence.

You see, we were all directors of *a nursing home*. A large one. A seven-acre senior care campus with a skilled nursing and rehabilitation center (sixty state-of-the-art guest rooms for patients right above my office); a large, assisted-living residential house; and two large memory care hacienda-style living spaces. As I noted, many in our meeting were clinicians, but there were other departments represented too. Directors included campus maintenance, dining services, business and sales, housekeeping, a horticultural guide, and my team—campus-wide programming and activities: community life.

We all had our official director titles, but my inside, unofficial title was *director of magical moments*. Bestowed one day early on by my fearless and beloved leader, Brenda, it has to be one of the all-time best job titles. My team (truly a dream team—four women, Lluvia, Gloria, Pati, and Chelsea—each more talented than the next) and I had shared so many magical moments over the past few years with these residents. All of them had become like family to us, as had the legions of staff members and care-givers who contributed each day and hour to making this a truly amazing, one-of-its-kind place. We even had two horses, Prissy and Herman, with their able wranglers, Anna and Carol, who were a hugely integral and beloved part of our community.

A SCREECHING HALT

Two weeks after the infamous stand-up/sit-down meeting, it was mid-March 2020, and the world as we knew it was completely turning upside down. Our team was asked to cancel everything—visitors from the outside and all our gatherings and events.

We had to call our favorite miniature mariachis (local young kids who get fully decked out in mariachi attire to play their tiny guitars and sing) and let them know they could not perform for us. We had to call and cancel the handsome Celtic singers who were going to be doing a presentation on the similarities between Bulgarian guitars and Celtic instruments (who knew, right?), celebrating St. Paddy's Day with us, and all the other fun, vibrant, and life-enhancing programs on our calendar.

Families were learning they could not visit their loved ones and were devastated, as were the loved ones, our residents, who were all being informed they would be confined to their rooms—indefinitely. There would, of course, be no meals in the dining rooms, no socialization. Nothing. Oh, and we all had to wear masks, no exceptions.

Working in a senior-care setting truly felt like being in the eye of the storm. Not only did we house people who were so vulnerable from a health standpoint, but we also had many residents in memory care who had no frame of reference whatsoever for what was going on. We were used to building morale through movement, action, doing things, and going places. It was head-spinning how quickly it all truly did come to a screeching halt.

The image of that red three-legged stool fit so well. It felt like all any of us could do was just sit around and wait. Maybe that was the big lesson. Were we all being given a massive timeout to learn about patience? This felt different from **it is what it is**, just accept it. Acceptance was a part of it, naturally, but there was a different **iiwii**. insight that emerged here. It was coming to terms with feeling stuck. We all were realizing we had to accept this COVID-19 storm with totally unknown outcomes, and yet we were learning to take a wait-and-see attitude. These were the conditions that existed, and somehow we had to make do.

Once we accept a situation, we usually have a choice of then taking action or not. Here, **iiwii**. suggests there might be wisdom in just letting things flow and take their course for a bit. It's natural to feel off-center, frustrated, and stuck when we feel like we're doing nothing. We realize it is sometimes OK *not* to feel OK. Although it felt like all our magical moments were over, we did decide to wait, as horribly uncomfortable as that was, to see what might emerge. Sure enough, it was in that stuck place of "sometimes I just sits" nothingness that an imperceptible something started to happen.

Maybe we could still create memorable moments, we realized, just ones that were very different from what we'd done before. They would involve more of a quiet, slow, "being with" our residents as opposed to the busy "doing and going" of our pre-pandemic days.

By sitting back and waiting, some unexpected offerings started to come to us, as if airdropped by some angels above working overtime. We learned quickly that there was some mask cartel that was hoarding masks for the masses, and we didn't have enough of them for our residents. I got a call from my friend Marianne, who asked if we'd be interested in some handmade masks that she had been sewing for a couple of people she knew.

I jubilantly replied, "Yes! And with fun, bright colors if you can get the fabric." About a week later, the first wave of masks showed up, in beautiful vibrant colors, patterns, and even some images like horses, dogs, golf clubs, and saguaros. We let each resident pick out a mask that resonated for them. The joy and delight of seeing everyone walk through the halls at a six-foot distance, waving at each other from their doors with their fun, bright masks on, was truly a shining light in the dismal dumpster of an existence we'd all been feeling.

My favorite interaction was when one of our memory care Alzheimer's residents came up and asked me for her "space rat." Hmmm. Her space rat? It took me a moment until I realized "space rat" sort of sounds like "face mask," which is exactly what she had meant. She got a lovely one with stars and planets!

We started to improvise on many fronts. Since we couldn't have the miniature mariachi kids visit, we could do a mariachi-themed door-to-door margarita cart with chips, salsa, and a few interesting varieties of margaritas—kumquat, rosemary, and basil—all with produce from our garden. We made do. From nothing came something extraordinary, as it turned out. We were tuning in to each other in new and different ways. And, yes, margaritas helped. I do note that most of the margaritas were virgin, but there were a few residents who had been given the OK for a little tequila. Tequila-infused or not, the marg cart was a huge spirit lifter.

Horse Hugs

AN UNEXPECTED VISITOR

We used whatever we had and allowed the pace to slow way down. When the horses would come and visit in the courtyards of the residents' haciendas, the residents could no longer come up and brush or be next to them. The magic of the horses was that just being in their presence, watching them from a distance, brought the same soothing experience of being up close and personal.

One day, however, we did get up close and personal. I had taken some time that morning just to be with the horses and have a few moments of quiet for myself. In typical **iiwii.** fashion, against all the voices of right/ wrong/shoulding in my head, something said, "Let today be different. Someone needs it to be."

Without really thinking much about it, I noticed that Herman, our inquisitive gelding (male-ish horse), kept insisting on walking toward one particular set of doors. Carol and Anna, our magnificent wranglers, noticed as well and fell right into line. Without a word being exchanged, somehow we were all tacitly on the same page—even both the horses. We got a bit bold, and Carol brought Herman right up to a resident's room that had two doors that opened up wide to the courtyard.

The resident, a dear soul named Joanie, who suffered from dementia, had absolutely loved her time with the horses but was bed-bound due to a hip fracture and not able to get outside. And so, we did it. We brought Herman right through the doors, into her room, onto her carpet, and up to her bed. He laid his huge, handsome chestnut-red head right on her chest. He was calm and knew he had a mission. She hugged him with her frail arms, and he hugged her back with his still, strong presence. She uttered some words to him under her breath and started to softly hum a tune. Herman closed his eyes, head on her chest, and just stood there motionless.

We had no idea what kind of interspecies dialogue we were witnessing, but something beautiful was communicated between both of these two beings. To an outside onlooker, other than a horse being in her room, it would have seemed like nothing much was going on. And yet in that nothingness, something profound happened—a sense of connection and love, a sense of being seen and touched. An afterglow of serenity and smiles was felt by all—even Herman as he slowly and carefully walked out of her room and back into the courtyard to tell Prissy all about it.

The pandemic is behind us now, and I am grateful. As our staff dwindled and the demands on those of us remaining multiplied, the exhaustion finally took its toll. The experiences of working literally in the trenches, side by side with other team members, have to mirror on some level what veterans feel returning from combat. It's hard to explain to anyone who wasn't there what it felt like to *be* there. While we sat and waited for things to gently start again, we had time just to go into a resident's room, pull up a chair, and let them tell us stories about their lives.

My favorite resident to visit was Luanne, and my favorite magical moment with her was when she shared her photo album with me, one very slow day of *doing nothing* together. She shared such fun photos of her family and places she'd visited, then she broke into a huge smile and said she had a surprise to show me. It was a photo and newspaper clipping of the new baby elephant that had just been born at our local zoo in early April 2020.

Luanne had been following the whole story and had let us all know when the little one finally arrived. It had just been named, she said, after 17,000 suggestions had been put forward during a citywide naming contest. She excitedly shared that the name selected for the adorable baby was to be Mapenzi. Talk about someone who embodied the bloom-where-you're-planted **iiwii.** essence. In the midst of total mayhem, she was focusing on the wonder and awe of the birth of a baby elephant at our zoo, whose new name meant "beloved" in Swahili.

Luanne then wanted to show me the last page of her album, which had a photo of our community life team. She said that we were her "beloveds," and she didn't know what she would have done without us. I told her that she probably just loved us for our kumquat-margarita door service and the bags of kettle corn we would smuggle in to her weekly. She just winked and carefully placed her album back on its shelf.

These moments that seem almost unremarkable in their simplicity, I realized, are the ones in which some of the strongest bonds are formed, which can imperceptibly become the stuff of lifetime friendships.

Along with these bonds, which curiously seemed to flourish in the space of less activity rather than more, there was something else that I also unexpectedly gained. It was a perspective of huge respect for the unsung heroes of an industry I never expected to be a part of but found myself inextricably tied to during this strange time in history. In the **iiwii.** space of doing nothing, slowing down, and taking it all in, I was able to make the following observation, discovered post-pandemic in my spiral notebook of random thoughts:

> *Many have been recognizing the "unsung heroes" as the frontline healthcare workers—the doctors, nurses, and clinical care teams. They are all the courageous healthcare workers who are working seemingly endless hours, experiencing levels of depletion that make my whining about exhaustion almost laughable. They know a part of their work, by nature and exposure,*

might be dangerous and health-compromising. With COVID-19, they are living this reality every moment. Truly, we all cannot say enough thanks to this dedicated group.

That said, the true heroes to me are what I am going to call the "second-line" workers. They are those who have been thrust into situations requiring every bit of (iiwii.) wisdom and fortitude that can be mustered. They are the people who are not remotely clinical, nor care to be, and did not sign up to be in situations where they might be exposed, among other things, to deadly viruses. They are not courageous in that way, like the frontline heroes are— and yet, in a way, they are even braver because they have chosen to stay once the pandemic hit and do their work nonetheless.

They are the housekeeping teams that have to clean up the rooms, bathrooms, and soiled clothes of those positive with COVID-19. They are the dining services teams that, round the clock, are trying to source, fix, and serve meals while supply chains are breaking down and they can no longer serve to central dining rooms. With all our residents confined to their rooms, hermetically sealed and plated portions of every single meal for every single resident in the community have to be individually assembled and delivered.

These people are the maintenance staff members who have to go into rooms that are teeming with the virus and change out a bed, fix an air conditioner, or replace a broken lamp (due to someone being so frustrated they slammed it against the wall). They are the people on teams like mine, community life, who have had the herculean task of keeping up morale, keeping our residents engaged, while sadness, boredom, and despair are seeping out from under every door.

Also among these second-line heroes is another easily forgotten group: the team members who have made the often excruciatingly hard and financially devastating decision not to be here but to be home right now with their *children, parents, and/or health-compromised family members because they know that they could not afford to come home and expose them to the COVID-19 virus.* [Written in the summer of 2020]

STUCK IN OVERDRIVE

I believe I speak for many when I say that being forced to stand still, "do nothing," and relinquish any and all control of life can be just as exhausting as being in perpetual motion. For some of us, it is even possibly more harrowing. So why is this **iiwii.** practice of doing nothing so hard? And why is it so important?

Here's a possible explanation for me: I started my professional career right around the same time the famous Nike "Just Do It" ad campaign was launched in the mid-1980s. Like many, I fully subscribed to this new religion of do-it-ism. I was working at the epicenter: New York City.

I found myself in this city (that never sleeps) of brand-new starts after having just gotten married to a wonderful man who is still my lifelong sidekick. I'd accepted a position at the once-iconic Eastman Kodak Company, working with international banks in all five boroughs of the city. At that time, I had zero clue what a borough was. I learned quickly. Covering all five boroughs was complete insanity. Nonetheless, I doubled down, buying fully into the "I want to make it here" mentality. Most days, I did not stop pounding the pavement or riding subways until I dropped. I literally got a stipend every month in my paycheck called "combat pay" to cover worn shoes, wrecked socks, ripped pantyhose—yes, we wore those back then, along with patent leather pumps—and subway tokens.

I share this not only to reveal the origins of my compulsion to not stop till I dropped but also to illustrate what the opposite of **iiwii.** looks like. It looks like frenetic doing and resulting exhaustion, the same burnt-out exhaustion referenced in the first sentence of this chapter: exhaustion when we frustratingly feel tired but cannot seem to settle our minds down long enough to actually even rest, much less sleep.

Bed of Rest??

My bed is a magical place where suddenly
I remember everything I was supposed to do.
—Anonymous

I love to sleep; it's sort of a hobby for me. Anything that disturbs this is annoying *and* is something worthy of figuring out and addressing. So this quest for understanding how, in essence, to shift gears from overdrive to neutral began way back then. Could the idea of slowing way down and Just (Don't) Do It actually be something to consider? It felt almost subversive.

Every ancient tradition has espoused this remedy of passive, regenerating inactivity (often overlooked by the perpetual-motion crowd) for pretty much everything. To be healthy, renewed, productive, etc., one must learn how to be still.

Martha Beck, another favorite author, who was both a fellow Arizonan and went to the same international business school I attended, insightfully and humorously adds another reason to subscribe to the **iiwii.** notion of doing nothing. She notes, "The problem is that perpetually doing, without ever tuning in to the center of our being, is the equivalent of fueling a mighty ship by tossing all its navigational equipment into the furnace. Fully occupied by the process of achieving innumerable goals, we lose the ability to determine which goals really matter and why."[1]

We also lose the capacity to even determine which *next steps* matter and might be helpful. When overload hits, learning to take ten to fifteen minutes each day to do what firefighters would call a "stop, drop, and roll" may actually be a shortcut to escaping the smoldering embers of a midday burnt-out brain.

So what is it, and how do we do it? How do we slow down (midday, mid-moment, or mid-life) and take a "do nothing" break?

Like with many things, sometimes the best way to define what something *is* is by defining what it *is not*. *Doing nothing*, the second integral practice of **iiwii.**, is not a nifty excuse to shirk the other responsibilities nipping at our heels. It is not a way to thumb our noses at something just because we don't want to do it. It is also not that nasty scourge—procrastination.

In her blog post entitled "Procrastination versus Percolation,"[2] Nisha Moodley points out that many of us often associate doing nothing with procrastination. She asks, "What if you're mislabeling your inaction," and it really is not inaction or doing nothing that is going on? Rather, she speculates, could it be that we are tapping into the power of percolation, giving ourselves the "time and space" for simmering, stewing, infusing, exploring, and taking mini vacations from *thinking* and *doing* so we don't end up running in a "straight line to nowhere"?

Understanding what it's not, here is what it is: doing nothing, as part of the **iiwii.** philosophy, is actually something that creates space so we *can* deal with all the doing, the tasks and responsibilities, possibly even more effectively.

As I've mentioned, I'm partial to bullet points and checklists. I have done my research and collected my own data. In my quest to successfully create a practice of doing a little bit of nothing every day, here is my own simple and tested practice:

1. Tune in body.
2. Tune out head.
3. Be still.

Our first objective is to turn our focus to the body; we tune in to our physical self. What's going on there? I often say that I live from the shoulders up. That's what I always notice right at first: my shoulders, neck, and head. Is there really a body down there? Sometimes, unless it's in pain, it's easy for me to forget there is.

Here, the challenge is actually to notice *all* parts of our body. Some say the ideal is to feel a full body tingle; get energy pulsing head to toe. A term I've learned describing this is somatic awareness; a way of tuning in so that we might feel what is actually going on. Do we feel easeful? Do we feel tense? Where do we feel relaxed, OK, and where do we hurt? Can we let ourselves reinhabit our body if in fact we possibly might have left it due to living in the upstairs head space? It might be missing us.

Next, now that the body is feeling felt, we get out of the headspace. Think of this time as a minivacation from ourselves, tuning out all mental ramblings for a period of time, say ten to fifteen minutes. Some squelch the head chatter by meditating and breathwork; some by using mindfulness apps or possibly just staring at the oasis emoji with the bright umbrella. I often do it by reading something. Something short and inspirational. Another great option I've found is simply to look at things and notice, with fresh eyes, what we actually see. It could be noticing the patterns formed by water dancing in a fountain, fire flickering off logs, or branches blowing in the breeze. Whatever the method, the key is to create a soft focus of the mind somewhere. Try this for a few minutes and then work up to longer.

Finally—and this is the most beautiful and possibly trickiest part of the process because we are so utterly not used to doing it—be still and listen.

This does not mean be still and still sneakily glance at our phone. It means finding someplace to be still, ideally with no noise. Hide where we cannot be found—a quiet, locked room is one option. Even better is going outside if we can get there.

> **The quieter you become, the more you are able to hear.**
> —Rumi
> (Persian poet, scholar and Sufi mystic, 1207–1273)

Rumi is one of my all-time ancient favorites, and his Sufi wisdom has been integral to my **iiwii** journey. Why is his notion of becoming quiet so foundational here for **iiwii.**? I have come to believe that it is when we are able to access a true acceptance mode, letting things be and then getting quiet and still, that an inner guidance system starts to subtly kick in. I call it IT: Inner Truth. It is a whisper that says, "Why not try this or that?" Some might call it a flash of insight or a tuning in to intuition. For others, it may be the "still, small voice of God." However we define IT for ourselves, if we are not quiet and listening, we will miss it.

Similar to the suggestion to view things afresh, not just looking but actually *seeing* what is in front of us, here **iiwii.** suggests we not only *listen* but learn how to *hear*. Listening is more like skimming the surface; we get caught up in words, the next thing we want to say, and distracting stories racing around in our minds. Hearing, like seeing, goes beyond the surface. It is taking in all that is being said and, often just as importantly, what is *not* being said. It gives us access to a deeper understanding.

This practice of stillness and hearing is a muscle we need to develop. It gets stronger and more impactful with practice. Curiously, this was the same thing my dad always used to say decades ago about our brain: "It is a muscle, honeygirl, and if it is used, challenged, and exercised, it will literally grow. And it will become stronger." We all have heard some version of this now, but at that point five decades ago, it seemed almost ridiculous. No one was referring to the brain as a muscle then, much less one you could do some sort of mental weight lifting with to get it in shape. At the time, I remember thinking it was a brilliant fabrication just to get me to do my homework.

Nonetheless, I complied. I understood even then that essentially he was saying we need to keep learning, even if it is (fifty years later) now learning how to slow down.

Ugh. I hate it when our dads are right.

A CALL TO REST

At its core, the idea of *doing nothing* is simply a *call to rest*. For many of us, it is a radical thought and, even more, a radical action (to allow for a state of inaction). We don't place much value on rest; we value results.

Catherine Meeks, PhD,[3] challenges the revolving door of doing, especially as it exists for people who don't have the luxury to opt out, even for a moment sometimes. She sees rest and slowing down as nonnegotiable necessities that we need to start taking very seriously. She goes so far as to call rest an "act of resistance," a phrase coined by Tricia Hersey.[4] This form of "resistance" is a radical act of intentionality.

Whether it is a right to rest or a compulsion toward ceaseless activity, where I come from, our worth is so often defined by how much we have gotten done: how quickly after a surgery we've gotten back on our feet, or how quickly after giving birth we are expected to be back at work—the superwoman or superman syndrome—none the worse for the wear. I recently learned that in some cultures, new mothers are required by their families and community to do nothing for forty days after the baby is born other than lie in bed or sit in a comfy chair, nursing the baby and being fed, massaged, and taken care of by everyone around her. What the heck? How did we stop doing that for each other and for our daughters?

Logjams 101

LOGJAMS

Whether we are a new mother juggling all the demands of caretaking a small human or anyone who feels like life has handed us more than we can handle, this mode of being constantly "on" and *doing* has become a universal experience. The endless streams of the to-do and to-be-done lists start manifesting as hundreds of small, bright post-it notes or, alternatively, a plethora of organizational apps that seem to create even more portals of places to be monitored. When we add the to-do lists to the emails to the text messages to the phone messages to the random other channels for incoming deal-with-it debris, life as we know it starts to feel more than a wee bit tangled and complex.

Pile those on with all the self- and other-directed shoulding discussed in the last chapter, and, yes, the mess gets bigger. When I find myself in this unpleasant state, often the visual of a logjam comes to mind—a very big and gnarly one. Since I live in Arizona, logjams are not a common occurrence, nor are the rivers that house them. Nevertheless, just for fun and since this topic of overwhelm was slightly starting to depress me, I did some research. I tapped into the mystical, all-knowing source—my laptop—"What is the definition of logjam?"

The Google Dictionary definition appeared top of the list (apparently they have created their *own* dictionary; who knew?):

Noun: **log-jam**[5]

1. a crowded mass of logs blocking a river
2. a situation that seems irresolvable

Then I checked the tried-and-true *Merriam-Webster*:

Noun: **logjam**[6]

1. a jumble of logs jammed together in a watercourse
2. deadlock, impasse
3. blockage
4. jam, crowd

I was then on a roll, so I extended the search to the *Collins English Dictionary* (I had never heard of it either) just for kicks:

Noun: **log jam**[7]

1. blockage caused by the crowding together of a number of logs floating in a river
2. a deadlock; standstill

Interestingly, I came up with some unexpected insights from my mini-research project on logjams. First, if you are an astute reader, you will notice that all three definitions spell *logjam* a different way. Fascinating.

Next, they all indicate a sense of stuckness, waiting for just the right push, shove, or unjumbling of the jumble so that the logs can move freely, once again, downriver. The goal for all these definitions is to get to a place of flow: unlock the deadlock. Get the standstill moving. Unjam the jammed-up crowd. Be the hero who resolves the irresolvable. A place of movement and flow—isn't that a space where we are all, by the way, supposed to get to?

I recently read a book entitled *Joyful Wisdom*, which had a chapter ingeniously entitled "The Problem Is the Solution."[8] So, to apply this concept: if the problem is that there's too much going on, and we are having a hard time getting to a place of acceptance and are experiencing our life (and shoulds) jamming up by the day, *and* there seems to be *nothing* we can do about it, then *why not practice doing nothing?* It's seriously ridiculous, right? And clearly counterintuitive. And yet, when I googled "How do you unjam a logjam?" I got an extraordinary answer. "To get it to flow, do nothing." Even if it looks "jammed," it is actually, imperceptibly, in flow, and basically, messing with it could make it worse. It could lose its flow.[9]

Be Still

Practice non-doing, and everything will fall into place.
—Byron Katie
(American author and speaker)

In a way, it all makes sense. If we want bread to rise, we leave it alone. If we are in the middle of intense negotiations, we stall for time. If we want the logs to unjam, apparently we just let the river do it for us and stay out of their (the logs') business. It's actually an argument, in a way, for supporting the proverbial path of least resistance, a path that often gets a bad rap. That path, of slowing down and letting things naturally take their course, is captured in some wonderful modern-day wisdom.

Barbara Fredrickson, from the University of North Carolina at Chapel Hill, has yet another reason for advocating do-nothingness. She has done extensive research around different ways of bringing a sense of positivity into our lives. She and her team discovered that *serenity* is the core emotion most closely linked to the urge to—guess what? Do nothing! She creates a beautiful description:

> It's when you let out that long, luxurious sigh because your current circumstances are so comfortable and so *right*. It's when you lie back in a shaded hammock after a day of strenuous and rewarding work in your garden. . . . It's strolling down a sandy beach on a bright morning with ocean sounds filling your head and a cool

breeze tingling your skin. . . . **Serenity** [emphasis mine] makes you want to sit back and soak it in. It's a mindful state that carries the urge to savor our current circumstances and find ways to integrate them into your life more fully and more often.[10]

She states that it is often referred to as the "afterglow emotion." Amazing. Just reading that description makes me want to go curl up in a comfy little ball somewhere and breathe deeply. My practice of doing nothing has yet to make it to the fifteen-minute mark, but one day perhaps I, too, will achieve this afterglow emotion.

An **iiwii.**-inspired *doing nothing* encourages us to enjoy a mode of just being, of stillness in order to reach a place of flow. As discussed in the last chapter, these concepts are far from new. Ancient wisdom has revealed this truth with beauty and clarity through the words of Lao Tzu, the Chinese philosopher (circa 500 BCE), who is known as the founder of Taoism. He stated that the Tao does nothing but leaves nothing undone.[11]

What we resist persists. Do an **iiwii**. Accept it first. Next, do nothing, and see what happens. Let the universe take a shot at figuring it out for us. Head for the beach and see what's unjumbled when we get back. Our friend Lao Tzu may be on to something. And so may Anne Lamott:

> *Lighthouses don't go running all over an island looking for boats to save; they just stand there shining.*
>
> —Anne Lamott, *Bird by Bird*
> (American novelist and essayist)

Just Shine

DO NOTHING (LET IT FLOW)

Horse Hugs

Bed of Rest??

Logjams 101

Be Still

Just Shine

4

Embrace Mystery

The most beautiful thing we can experience is the mysterious.
It is the source of all true art and science.

—Albert Einstein
(German mathematician and physicist, 1879–1955)

"Do You Want to Be Cousins or Not?"

I continue to be amazed at the zillions of things we can learn online in an instant. Just like the fruitful quest to unearth information about log jams/log-jams/logjams in the last chapter, my next inquiry yielded equally fruitful results. Providing context for this next story, my research this time was about the history of a common, yet odd, phrase "Don't look a gift horse in the mouth."

Its earliest reference is believed to be from a Latin text of St. Jerome, *The Letter to the Ephesians*, circa CE 400, which contains the text "*Noli equi dentes inspicere donati*" ("Never inspect the teeth of a horse that's been given to you"). Flash forward to 1546, and apparently a man named John Heywood translated this phrase into the Middle English lexicon and sent it on its way to renown.

Embrace Gifts

No man ought to looke a geuen hors in the mouth.
—John Heywood
(English author, poet, and playwright, 1497–1580)

Don't look a gift horse in the mouth. Now that we have its context, what does it mean? This phrase is well past its prime—or, for many, its relevance—and yet it still exists. Roughly, it encourages us, when something good happens—a gift of sorts lands in our lap—to be grateful rather than analytical.

Here is an example by way of its original use: A horse is gifted to us, and so we open its mouth and check the teeth because teeth determine the health and the age of a horse. We then decide if we really want this horse or if we just want to give it back. Horses are expensive to maintain, even healthy ones, so if the teeth appear bad or old, the deal is often off. It's time to pull up the trailer and say goodbye to what might have been: other than a broken tooth or two, a perfectly good horse or one that was sick. Is this an opportunity missed or a mishap dodged? We will never know. Either way, the gifted horse is gone.

To broaden the visual to a more esoteric level, how many times do we completely overlook something wonderful that is staring us right in the face and instead decide we need to spend hours, maybe days, or even years essentially "checking its teeth" or figuring it out first?

I come from a family that almost completely blew the chance of a lifetime because of this ingrained—and, for many Americans, hard-wired—curse: the relentless need for *definition*. The story entitled "Do You Want to Be Cousins or Not?" could easily constitute its own novel. It is one of my absolute favorite parts of our family lore as it combines so many different threads of history happening during an epically difficult yet important era. Taking place during the late 1930s into the 1940s, it is a tale of two families, separated by an ocean, who shared the same last name and a world that was falling apart. But first, some background.

My family comes from Quaker stock, often known for having a very strong penchant for proof: getting things just right and nailed down. My grandmother Marjorie grew up in Dayton, Ohio, and then moved to Kansas City, Missouri, for high school. She loved to ride horses and play sports. She was very athletic, excelling at competitive tennis at a time when women wore tennis dresses that went down to their ankles. She was nationally ranked and won several tournaments all around the Midwest in the early 1900s. She was fearless and definitely would have been a teeth checker if anyone tried to gift her a horse. You won her affection by proving yourself worthy. She kept a ledger that recorded every dollar she ever spent and wrote in a small five-lined journal every day. Marjorie was disciplined, formidable, and suffered no fools. She was especially proud of her family, her heritage, and her extensive genealogical charts.

It was the mid-1930s, and my grandmother was no doubt like many who were at their wits' end, trudging their way through the trials and tribulations of the Great Depression (1929–1939) only then to be smacked with the infamous "black blizzards" of dust that were decimating the Midwest, adding to the hardships of an already very harsh decade. It was called the Dust Bowl, and for those who could, the solution during that bleak time was just to get the hell out of Dodge (a town in Kansas, by the way) if you had the means to do so. The goal was to get as far away as you could to escape the punishing elements, something most people at the time had no means to do.

To further set the stage, my grandmother was married to John ("Jack") Bailey Gage, a Kansas Citian who, through an unusual set of circumstances, had been approached in the late 1930s to run for mayor against an incumbent backed by one of the worst political-machine bosses of the twentieth century. My grandfather was seriously contemplating putting his law practice on hold so he could take the time needed to lead a grassroots effort to oust Tom Pendergast and his corrupt crew of cronies and mobsters. Meanwhile, my grandmother and my mom's family were embedded right in the midst of it all too—lots of heat and dirt, both polit-ical and otherwise, for everyone. There was no option for them to get the hell out of Dodge or anywhere else for that matter. They were stuck.

CHANCE MEETING IN THE DOWNS

During this time, some friends of Marjorie and Jack decided to travel far away to a land where dust was not blowing—back to the motherland, England, for some quiet rest and relaxation in the countryside. These family friends cruised to their destination via one of the ocean liners of the day—possibly the RMS *Queen Mary*, just to set the stage. Remember, these were times with no cross-Atlantic flights, no Airbnbs, no internet, no cell phones. You would just stumble out into the unknown and see what places and adventures you found or which ones found you. Travel back then was an adventure in embracing mystery on a whole different level. And mystery is what these friends of my grandparents returned to Kansas City with—a curious interaction they had experienced while deep in the downs of Sussex, England.

As told to me, through handed-down bits of stories, these over-seas-traveling friends, on their eventual return home, apparently shared something like the following with my grandparents Marjorie and Jack: "We have the most extraordinary news! There is someone named Gage who looks just like you, Jack, a spittin' image who lives in Sussex, England, just south of London."

I may be using some creative license here with the dialogue, but this was probably close. (By the way, *spittin' image* was one of hundreds of weird colloquial familial phrases I grew up with. Many, like this one, seem to make no sense whatsoever when you really think about them. Why would we spit on an image? Maybe to clean up a dirty mirror so we can see ourselves?)

The normal reaction to news like this would most likely be a polite shrug and an appreciative smile, which Jack probably did. The formi-dable Marjorie Gage, however, probably was thinking a skeptical "Oh, *really?*" (or something more pointed) with a well-practiced grimace of subtle superiority.

The plot then thickened. Their friends shared that this supposed doppelganger named Gage was not a "mister." He was a *lord*, also known in the verbiage of the English nobility as a *viscount*. Christened Henry Rainald Gage, he was part of a long line of Gages who had owned an ancestral home called Firle Place, along with a number of adjoining villages, for several hundred years. Apparently, he owned quite a few pieces of art and a large number of sheep. My grandfather's true passion was farming and raising livestock, so this would have absolutely piqued his interest.

So back to Marjorie, who has been gutting it out through the Depression, Dust Bowl, and raising four young children with a husband contemplating running for office against the mob. This all must have added up to a hefty handful at the time. There were two rambunctious boys, John and Frank; an older stepdaughter, Betty Lane; and then came Anne, my mother. Imagine a very energetic, tomboyish-like girl (think Scout from *To Kill a Mockingbird*) constantly in trouble, trying to keep up with her brothers. She was probably the opposite of the kind of daughter a Quaker mother might have hoped for and probably contributed to my grandmother's ever-growing grimaces.

All of this provides a backdrop to the state of mind I imagine my grandmother might have been in when she experienced the Henry-Rainald-Gage-the-lord-whom-we-met-on-our-trip-to-England conversation. Of course, this was *way* before there was anything resembling the internet, as previously mentioned. Information about people around the world was communicated by letters or telegrams or through anecdotes, colorful little stories, and quips about interesting "foreigners" and nobility. These were exactly the kinds of things that someone might share with people they are trying to impress. The conversation, I imagine, continued something like this: "Well, Jack, the ancestral house, called Firle, is lovely and very large. There is a portrait on the wall of one of the staircase landings of a previous Lord Gage, apparently there have been several, and, as we said, he looks just like you. We could not wait to get back and tell you about this. And you are not the only one who is excited. The lord wanted us to give you his full name and address. He even suggested that your families might *possibly* be related; perhaps you are distant cousins?"

As my mother, tomboy Anne, shared her version of the story with me, my grandfather apparently was instantly smitten with this tale. Marjorie? Not so much. As my mom said, "Can you imagine Grandmother's reaction?" Many people, then as now, were skeptical of unsubstantiated "too good to be true" scenarios around these sorts of things, and my grandmother would have been in a category all her own.

Marjorie Hires Gage was not going to simply *claim to be related* to someone just because they shared the same last name and similar looks. One had to do their due diligence with these sorts of things. Intricate genealogical charts had been created for just this kind of investigation, which is, I'm sure, how she saw it: a mystery to be solved, a puzzle to be pieced together, not just something to accept at face value.

If only she could have known and had the ability at her fingertips to find out who this family was, to solve this puzzle. *If only* she could have typed a little question into an all-knowing, yet-to-be-invented keyboard (resembling a flattened typewriter) in 1939 and asked, "What is this Firle Place in Sussex, England?" If she hypothetically could have performed such wizardry, here is something close to what she might have found:

A COUNTRY ESTATE IN THE SOUTH DOWNS NATIONAL PARK

Firle Place is an outstanding privately owned country house in Sussex that dates from the time of Henry VIII, but which was substantially remodeled during the Georgian period. Firle Place is very much a family home which provides the perfect setting to house an exemplary collection of works of art, fine furniture and porcelain of national significance.

The family's 500-year history at Firle started when Sir John Gage (1479–1556) built his great Tudor manor house, which appears to have been completed circa 1543.

Incorporating several villages and farms spread over rolling hills, the Firle Estate, in the heart of the magnificent South Downs

National Park, is just 60 miles from London. Firle illustrates a rare cultural continuity with an unusually intact estate and a thriving rural community. Central to the atmosphere is Firle's diverse and culturally rich community with many artists, craftsmen, and local businesses.[1]

Moving on to modern (1930s and onward) times, here is when our Henry Rainald (commonly referred to only as Rainald) and his crew come on the scene:

Henry Rainald attended Eton College and was on the verge of going to Oxford when the war broke out. He joined the Coldstream Guards and went to France early in 1915 and was invalided out in 1917 having been hit by shrapnel. In 1931 Henry Rainald married the Hon. Imogen Grenfell, daughter of Lord and Lady Desborough of Taplow House and Panshanger in Hertfordshire, inheriting part of the celebrated collection of both houses in 1952.

Together they re-arranged the rooms at Firle, and Henry Rainald continued to take a great interest in the collection. His great contribution was his leadership of the campaign to preserve the South Downs from growing development, and as a result of his efforts as Chairman of East Sussex County Council the area eventually came to be designated an Area of Outstanding Natural Beauty and, long after his death, a National Park.

His two sons succeeded him in turn, George John (known as Sammy) (1932–1993) became the 7th Viscount, and Henry Nicholas (b. 1934) (HG5) is the 8th Viscount, and Camilla Jane (b.1937). Henry Nicholas lives at Firle today with his family, where he manages the estate and is an artist.[2]

The title of viscount has accordingly been handed down now as new generations are taking the helm, but otherwise, Firle's stateliness and beauty have remained constant. Whether looking it up one hundred years ago or today, the content probably has not changed much regarding the description of the Firle ancestral home and certainly not regarding the early history of the Gage family.

Additionally, with yet another Google inquiry, we could read about Charleston on the Firle estate, referenced earlier in part one, which housed the collective artistic crew of Vanessa Bell, Duncan Grant, Virginia Woolf, and the heralded Bloomsbury Group.

The point of all this is that yes, if Marjorie had known the back story, the rich history of Firle, and the many interesting people and facets associated with this place and this family, just the notion of being related and referred to as cousins (whether provable then or not) would have felt like an unabashed honor. But she knew none of this.

And so back to the conversation my grandparents had with their friends the overseas travelers. Not only did Lord Gage supposedly think they *might* be related, but the friends furthermore declared, "Lord Gage apparently would like to correspond with you. He was especially interested after we told him about what you've been doing. He insists you write him as soon as possible."

A TRANSATLANTIC PEN PAL

It was late 1939, and Jack and Marjorie had been getting into full gear for the risky and difficult mayoral election in Kansas City the following spring. The pen-pal arrangement had been fully embraced and was apparently becoming an important conduit of information and source of support for both Jack and Lord Gage. Not only did they apparently discuss their passions about raising cattle and sheep; they also kept each other updated on what was happening during this petrifying time of unknowns in their respective communities and countries.

While Jack was busy campaigning, there was much going on, and often it was not good. In fact, it was yielding some unexpected ugly and harsh consequences for his family. The Pendergast "machine" controlled the police force, the sanitation department, and all construction contracts in the city, just to name a few. My grandparents did not have their trash collected for a year. There were bricks thrown through windows and most incredulous of all, there were death threats made against the children. Fortunately and thankfully however, as election time was approaching, the state governor stepped in and passed emergency legislation placing the control of the police department under the state, not local city government.[3] This was an instrumental shift in swaying Jack's decision to finally run for mayor. Although the threats did not go away, at least there was now protection. My mother, who was in about fifth grade then was finally able to be escorted by police officers to walk half a block to her school, Bryant Elementary.

As all this was going on with my people in Kansas City, across the Atlantic, Lord Gage's family was dealing with its own form of a different sort of mounting danger and hardship. Europe was in upheaval. Germany had invaded Poland on September 1, 1939, and immediately after, the United Kingdom and France declared war on Germany, with specific aims to curtail the unfettered aggression of the Nazi leader, Adolph Hitler.

It was at this point that all the various threads of this family story come together to underscore the huge leap of faith it takes to jump into the mystery of the unknown, accepting uncertainty and doing what we feel needs to be done. Exemplifying a profound and difficult act of **iiwii.**, this leap came in the form of either a letter or quite possibly a telegram in the spring of 1940. From resignation and anger to acceptance of the severity of the situation, a very sincere offer was made. It was sent directly to Rainald from my grandparents, Jack and Marjorie. I imagine it went something like this: "If you can get your children on a ship before the bombing starts, they are welcome to come live with us and our family in Kansas City. They can stay as long as necessary—until it's safe enough for them to return back home to England. Hopefully we can all take care of this madman Hitler and get things sorted out so that this does not escalate."

Timing is a strange thing. Why is it often during utter chaos that some of our most important life requests land quietly on our doorstep? Jack and Marjorie realized there was a need, one that transcended the temporary mayhem they were experiencing right then and opened their arms. Rainald and his family responded with a heartfelt and resounding "Yes. Let's try this." It was agreed that the three children (all under ten years old at the time) from Firle—Sammy, Camilla, and Nicky—would be coming to Kansas City to live with my mother and her family for whatever span of time would be needed.

TORPEDOES

The arrangements had all been made, and the transatlantic tickets had been purchased for the overseas voyage to America. The three children were en route to the docks to board their ship when they got the news: German bombers were approaching England. News of potential bombings was being broadcasted, and they heard that the ship that set sail just prior to their outgoing vessel had just been torpedoed. As a result, no one was boarding any ships to go anywhere, and the three Gage children ended up waiting out the next few years of the war not in Kansas City but tucked into remote parts of the English countryside, where many families fled for safe shelter.

I was fortunate to exchange email communications with Camilla Gage (a.k.a. Lady Camilla Jane Cazalet) in September 2022, in which she shared her memories of this time: "I remember Cousin Jack and Cousin Marjorie tremendously well and with huge affection. They were wonderful. (We may well not be cousins, but you all FEEL like first cousins!) During the war they sent us loads of food parcels and in 1940/41 or/42 offered to take the three of us to Kansas City for the duration of the war; we were all set to go with passports at the ready when the ship before ours was torpedoed and my parents decided the crossing would be too hazardous. So we stayed put. (Sadly, I would have loved to have come!)"

The question of being officially "related" was no longer relevant. Our families became connected in a way that transcended the need for definition. Lord Gage's impactful remark in one of his many letters to Jack—"Ask Marjorie, do you want to be cousins or not?"—had been answered.

What I love about this story is that it was with sincere concern and without hesitation that Marjorie and Jack offered that the children could come over and stay as long as was needed. They would be welcomed as family. *As family*. No need for genealogical charts, lineages, dates, and places of origin. No need for proof of anything.

After the war was over, Jack and Rainald finally got to meet in person. The Gages of Kansas City and the Gages of Firle officially claimed each other as "cousins," and, for decades since, we have all been visiting each other, back and forth, making many of our own transatlantic trips. Then and now, we continue to embrace the mystery and magic of this amazing relationship. In ways more important than any Ancestry.com connection could ever create, a new line on both of our family trees had been hand-drawn in—with permanent ink.

LET GO OR BE DRAGGED

Like both sets of Gage families experienced, often we find we simply have no choice but to let things go and relinquish control over situations we'd desperately love to control. "Let it go." We hear this phrase so often, but recently I saw the added "or be dragged" part and thought it perfectly appropriate for **iiwii**. It's hard to let go of what we think is the right or appropriate thing to do. Getting all dots to connect pristinely feels so good. The reality is that life doesn't like to behave that way. And the real kicker is that, if you decide you do not want to let go of a situation, there quite often can be some rugged dragging that goes on.

We've discussed the initial theme of **iiwii.**, which is, first, to accept. We work through the resignation, resistance, and even through the stress responses of freeze, fight, or flight. Sometimes we experience the **iiwii.** moment of *snap out of it*. Sometimes we don't. The **iiwii.** way suggests that we let it be.

We then move into a counterintuitive theme of *let it flow* by learning how to make it a practice to do nothing, a monumentally simple yet difficult feat for many of us in these times. By waiting it out, letting things percolate, letting metaphorical logs untangle themselves on the river of our life, we see what may emerge on its own to possibly remedy or resolve a tricky situation.

Finally, we learn the importance of understanding **iiwii.** through one last realm—the embracing of mystery. It is accepting that not everything ties neatly together, and actually that can be not only OK but possibly even brilliant in the end. This is what Marjorie did as she opened her home to these lovely people from England who were trying, like everyone else, to creatively navigate the uncertainties of a world at war.

This is what Jack had to do when saying yes to running for mayor, something that literally put everyone he loved at risk, all in an effort to do what he felt was nonnegotiable: help the city that he loved to get back on what he and many others felt was a track of integrity. Which, by the way, he did in a heroic way. His legacy and impact were profound, being cited years later as one of the most important US mayors of the twentieth century for his cleanup and reform of Kansas City's post-Pendergast, corruption-riddled city government. As an aside, fortunately their trash finally did start getting picked up again, and my mom at last could walk to school on her own—without police protection.

MYSTERY—THE SPICE OF LIFE?

As I was pondering all the various facets of this story, it led me to further inquiries and research around the concept of mystery. A huge surprise was finding that one of the greatest scientific minds of all times, Albert Einstein, was captivated by this concept of mystery, which, ironically, seems to be the exact opposite of the hard data-driven mentality most scientists seem to have. Many have seen his poignant quote cited at the beginning of this chapter, and yet as I sourced it later, I found out it was incomplete. The full version of the quotation is as follows: "The most beautiful thing we can experience is the mysterious. It is the source of all true art and science. He to whom this **emotion** [my emphasis] is a stranger, who can no longer pause to wonder and stand rapt in awe, is as good as dead: his eyes are closed."[4]

What I love about Einstein's last sentence is his use of the idea of mystery—the mysterious as an *emotion*. Like all emotions, it can run the full gamut of expression from lovely curiosity and intrigue on one end of the mystery-as-emotion continuum to full-blown anger and resentment at the other end.

Going one step further on the idea of mystery as emotion, in an article entitled "Psychology: A Sense of Mystery May Be the Spice of Life," author Scott Smith asserts that "the sense of mystery may be one of the most powerful emotions of all." He goes on to state,

> A sense of a mystery is like no other feeling. It seems to light up the brain in a unique way. It is hard to describe the emotion, but it is clear that people enjoy the feeling. . . . We humans like to figure things out and when there is not an apparent answer to something we like to look deeper to find out what is really going on. In a way, the sense of mystery may be one of the most powerful emotions of all.[5]

How does the brain create it, and how do we feel it? What does a sense of mystery compel us to do? What are the actual emotions comprising a sense of mystery?

Discover

"Mystery seems to be a complex emotional blend of curiosity, a desire to learn, a yearning to find out the answer. It lies behind all of human-kind's greatest accomplishments like going to the moon, discovering new energy sources, and exploring new [frontiers]."[6]

Embracing mystery can be very scary terrain to step into for almost everyone at different points in our lives. It means venturing into the unknown. It means we might have to open ourselves and our views just a bit more than we are comfortable doing. We might worry about the optics—what will others think? We worry we may fail, that we may get ourselves into something over our heads. It is just so much easier to cling to the known, the status quo, the path of least resistance. Such stories ("*we can't possibly do *that*"*) are commonplace and passed down to us, lovingly or not, through our ancestral DNA.

The author of a fun little book that was gifted to me years ago from a hometown (Kansas City) author, *Creating a Charmed Life*, has a beautiful description of the light, wonder-filled side of the emotion of mystery:

Be Amazed

Don't educate yourself out of the elation of being genuinely amazed.
—Victoria Moran
(American author, speaker, and spiritual adventurer)

Choosing to take a step, especially when we have no clue where it will take us, is the ultimate act of embracing mystery. It is what our ancestors have been doing for centuries. It is what Jack and Marjorie had to do: take steps to go out on a limb that could have broken off at any moment. If either of them had spent too much time overthinking what was going on, the elation of truly being amazed by what ultimately ended up being positive outcomes easily might have been doused.

No destination is ever absolutely knowable, even if we do our best to plan it. One minute we're planning to put our children on a ship bound for destinations to live with people completely unknown, and the next thing we know, bombers are on their way, and the ship that set off just yesterday has been torpedoed and sunk. Our Gage cousins from Firle had to let go of their meticulously crafted plans. Otherwise, an unutterably sad outcome might have occurred. They let themselves be open to the unfolding, realizing, as everyone was at that point, that the illusion of control over anything was being shattered right and left.

Moving into the space of **iiwii.** offers us the serenity and peace that come from hunkering down. We allow ourselves to get quiet, go inward, and shut the door to the chaos of the world for a while. It is like giving the seedling time to grow in the darkness of the soil, uncertain if it will ever get to break through and feel the light. We learn through slow navigation, reading the way, step by step—setting sail or fleeing into the hills. When we cling too closely to outcomes and the way we think things *should* be going, life certainly can drag us through lots of mud. It's easier and cleaner at times just to let go.

No Right/Wrong

Out beyond ideas of wrongdoing and rightdoing there is a field.
I'll meet you there.

—Rumi

(Persian poet, scholar and Sufi mystic, 1207–1273)

Uncertainty is certain. Realizing we often have zero control over much of anything is, to say the least, disturbing. It's not about what is right or what is wrong. It is about embracing what is and the complexity and/or simplicity therein. Simply put, we just don't get to know how things are going to play out until they do. And often it can be in a way we never might have imagined.

So engage in the emotion of mystery, be it full of awe or full of awfully tough unknowns. Be patient. Be brave. See what gradually surfaces, and, lo, we might find ourselves being embraced by charming "cousins" who truly *do* become family, scattered up and down the downs of the exquisite coastal English countryside.

EMBRACE MYSTERY (LET IT GO)

Mystery as Art, Science

Embrace Gifts

Discover

Be Amazed

No Right/Wrong

5

Transformation: iiwii.
Ancestral Ahas

What we cultivate in times of ease,
we store up to support in times of change.
—Buddha (c. 563–483 BCE)

The Great Learning

I'm not even sure why the phrase *ancestral ahas* keeps surfacing for me, but nonetheless, I'll use it. Maybe it's the alliteration. In tying together the concept of **iiwii.**, several ahas have emerged. I'm collectively calling them the Great Learning—a phrase that feels a bit bold and yet feels appropriate. Several of these insights have to do with a way of being that has been very foreign to my particular ancestral line.

In **iiwii.**, we are being called to rest, to cultivate stillness and ease, to go with the flow. We are being asked, without resentment, resistance, or resignation, to simply accept a situation. **it is what it is.**

Once upon a time, I would have been laughed right out of my lineage for advocating this perspective. I am the descendant of Protestants, pilgrims, pioneers, Quakers, and Depression-era people. I am also the daughter, niece, and granddaughter of their offspring, which included an array of attorneys, doctors, veterinarians, farmers, business owners, and engineers—not a super low-bar group. All of these women and men, up and down my DNA strand, were known for their work ethic: Don't stop till you drop. Time is money. You are what you do. Fail to plan, plan to fail. And so on. Contemplating your navel (a.k.a. self-reflection) was considered a nonsensical waste of time. To consider the use of concepts like letting it be and flow, or to say we are pulling a wabi-sabi or an uketamo(w) to help us navigate our journeys would have been unheard of with this crowd.

As a baby boomer, I think I can speak for our entire generation when I say that, for example, we love the iconic Beatles song "Let It Be," and yet we have no clue how to apply those lyrics to our own lives. Switching into **iiwii.** mode is not as simple as it seems it would be. Sitting around and doing nothing, for many of us, is just not in our generational DNA. This explanation nails it:

> The phrase "be here now" calls to mind images of bearded stoners in bell-bottomed pants, utterly relaxed about whatever's happening around them. Yet in fact the attempt to be here now feels not so much relaxing as rather strenuous—and it turns out that trying to have the most intense possible present-moment experience is a surefire way to fail. . . . Making the deliberate effort to appreciate life's smaller pleasures—it turns out to be bewilderingly difficult to do.[1]

When I mentioned—in a hushed voice, after a few glasses of wine—this book project to a close friend, he opened up, in an equally hushed voice, and shared that, in fact, he had just written his own book. He said it is the only one-word book, he believes, in existence. The word is—maybe you guessed it—"BE."[2] Gradually, our generation is starting to get it. And yet much work and learning still need to be done.

EVOLUTIONARY

The three themes supporting **iiwii.**—acceptance, do nothing, embrace mystery—are stereotypical of what I believe we Westerners often think of as traditionally "Eastern" philosophies. An interesting thing happened, though, that upended this premise of mine. I asked a friend of Eastern culture, a beautifully brilliant young Filipina woman named Patricia, to do an early reading of the book, and we then discussed my references (a.k.a. stereotyping) of Eastern and Western cultures. In sharing with her how I felt we have so much to learn from concepts like kintsugi, wabi-sabi, and the stereotypical Zen approach to a more laid-back way of living, I got a surprising response. She simply asked, "Have you not heard about tiger moms?"

She challenged my simple siloing, as she should have, and revealed that she and many of her fellow Easterners feel that our Western culture is far more laid back, open, and go-with-the-flow than theirs, with its ever-increasing high bar for unremitting excellence. Another ancestral aha. A new learning to replace an outdated stereotype.

In my experience with what I am or was defining as our Western mindset, I realized that whoever it is we are, we have trouble understanding things that cannot be proven. If we can't think it, know it, sense it with our brain, or touch it, then it does not exist. The **iiwii.** philosophy asks us to reconsider this approach. Concepts of acceptance and accepting our limitations—making margaritas with the ingredients at hand, dealing with cave-induced panic attacks and accepting unsolvable cousin mysteries—need to replace the well-worn and grooved path that asserts that "this is *unacceptable* and needs to remedied immediately."

I think many would agree that we've done an admirable job of developing the mind (thinking) but often to the detriment of the heart (feeling). For centuries, especially in what I *will* call Western medicine, the mind has been seen as matter—nothing more, nothing less. "I think, therefore I am" (thank you, Mr. Descartes). The mind goes; we go. Typically, from this mindset, the brain has *not* been traditionally recognized as a conduit for unseen data, for wisdom, and possibly even for long-internalized trauma from past generations to emerge. Gradually, we are learning in this area too.

In the book *An End to Upside Down Thinking*, author Mark Gober challenges this entire line of "thinking." He stresses that our brain houses our consciousness, which is not only collective and interconnected but also timeless. It lives within and yet beyond the confines of the cells in our head, which we have been trained to believe are all tangibly housed within our skull. This consciousness is not confined by conventional notions of how we understand time, space, and reality to work together. It is not tangible.

For me, the image that pops to mind is a type of Ethernet—a frequency or Wi-Fi channel that picks up data from external sources, not just the endless minutiae we conjure up in our moment-to-moment life commentaries. It picks up circuits of invisible happenings, instructions, and data flowing all around us. If we can't see, for example, the multitudes of radio waves or internet and cell-frequency bands that exist invisibly, bouncing all around us, then what else are we not seeing?

Maybe this flow is like a conduit of ancient/new information that is accessible to us when we are being still—tuning in and listening. If we don't tune in and intentionally make an effort to access it, then it is gone. If we don't pray the prayer, the gift of the answer may not be received. This is essential **iiwii.** stuff.

Years ago, I heard a story from US Senate Chaplain Richard Halverson that forever changed the way I look at and consider the importance of prayer. It initially seemed like a quasi-pointless tale, which ended up having a game-changing message.[3]

Here is the SparkNotes version: Person dies, goes to heaven, and meets St. Peter at the gate. They go on a tour. All looks as one would expect, except for a "large, cavernous warehouse" stuffed to the gills with boxes, letters, and large envelopes addressed to multitudes of random people. Tour ends. Peter asks new heavenly entrant if there are any questions. Person replies, "Yes, a big question. Everything looked exactly as I dreamed it would except for that massive building that looked like a postal service for the residents up here. Do we get mail from our loved ones?"

St. Peter replies, "No, dear soul, you do not get mail here. You get so much more but not mail. "This huge warehouse, is filled with every imaginable size of box, letter, and package each containing something of great importance and value—the answers to prayers that have never been asked."

Confused, the new resident replies, "You mean there is something we have to do to have these answers sent?"

"Yes," says St. Peter. "You see, often it is before we even have the need, much less have asked the prayer, that God has the answers ready and waiting. For them to be delivered, all that is required is one thing, that someone simply makes the request."

With **iiwii.**, from a place of stillness and quiet, we are being encouraged to remember to make the request, set the intention, pray the prayer. Get specific, if that's possible (and sometimes it's not) for what we want to have happen either to us or for our loved ones. Then relax. In this case, it is not about fixing or solving things ourselves, applying Herculean effort to make something work. It is about letting go, being patient, and seeing what answer may arrive one day on our own doorstep. (And remember, if the package is empty, that may be our answer, too.)

While these notions may sound possibly intriguing or possibly ridiculous, many of us, like my grandmother Marjorie Gage, would likely have fallen toward the more skeptical side. We crave definition. We like data over spongy theories. Seriously, is there really something (or someone) listening to our prayers and requests? We need tangible proof of everything—until we don't. Until we learn to embrace what can't be seen or heard and yet simply know in our heart exists. We need this sense of definition and proof until some faraway mysterious "cousins" come along who say otherwise.

These are wobbly times. We are all being taught, whether we want to be or not, the art of waiting and being patient with the discomfort of uncertainty. Learning to "do an **iiwii.**" is something that calls to me more and more. It brings to mind one last concept before we end part one, which is a beautiful notion from the Celtic tradition called *liminal space*. *Liminal* is a word I've always been intrigued by. It is defined as "on the threshold" or in a state "characterized by ambiguity and openness." A friend shared the following with me that a colleague of hers had written up and given her:

We experience liminal space when we are betwixt and between.

When the tried and true, which worked so well for so long . . . sometimes slowly, sometimes in fits and starts, sometimes suddenly . . . stops working. Leaving the familiar, without knowing the shape or contour of our next destination, we enter the Threshold of Liminal Space.

Uncertainty, anxiety and confusion often follow as the old routines no longer work, and we don't have any new practices or formulas to replace them. Holding the liminal space is challenging, but inside its chamber is truly where we are at our most teachable. It is in the liminal space that we are actually willing to rearrange our lives and make serious changes, because the threshold is so . . . uncomfortable![4]

PEARLS OF WISDOM

I struggled for years to make sense of why I could not shake the generic **iiwii** phrase and this quasi-obsession with the notion of acceptance or nonacceptance. Over and over, I just kept thinking, "This is 'irritating' or 'incredibly irritating.'" And then it hit me one day: maybe I could use irritation as fuel.

Here we go again with the problem becoming the solution. There is an irritant, something that feels uncomfortable that we'd like to shake, remove, demolish, and/or get rid of, but often, for reasons unknown, we cannot. It is like the grain of sand that finds its way into an open, unsuspecting oyster. Yes, maybe I could use the analogy of the pearl as a way of understanding this **iiwii.** irritation.

As much as the oyster might want to spit out this unwelcome tiny irritant, it decides to do an **iiwii.** and just let it be. Without any doing, just by being with this irritating foreign body that has lodged into its previously peaceful inner world, the oyster embraces the sand and lets it marinate. It lets things flow a bit. It doesn't *really* accept the sand, but it tries. It starts to coat it to remove the irritation, then keeps on coating it, actually making the pearl grow instead of rejecting it. After a while, it forgets that the irritating element is there, until lo and behold, one day, the piece of sand mysteriously has become the pearl—exquisite and lovely.

The oyster lets it be, and transformation has happened. With **iiwii.**, we find less is more. By not interfering and just accepting the situation as is, at least for now, and embracing the mystery of what might become, we quite possibly get to experience a new aha—an irritant becomes a pearl. The situation transforms and evolves into something altogether different from what we might have ever imagined.

In her book *Untamed*, Glennon Doyle shares the huge aha she had around the power of being still and learning how to trust what she refers to as "the Knowing." For me, it is my "inner **iiwii.**" Both point to the importance of cultivating stillness. It is from this place that eventually the answer, or what I call Inner Truth, emerges. She writes her own recipe for how to access this Knowing, which has inspired me to do the same:

Inner iiwii. from *Book of iiwii*

Irritating situation presents itself.

And now: it is what it is. Accept it.
Tune in body; move.
Feel → Tingle

Not now: do nothing.
Tune out mind; soft focus.
Look → See

For now: embrace the mystery of all that is unknown.
Be still; get quiet.
Listen → Hear

Let inner truth emerge.
(Or, simply revel in the peaceful moment.)

LOOSE ENDS

How often do we roll our eyes at quick fixes, simplistic metaphors, and yes, even *pearls* of wisdom? The question that always comes to mind for me is

"How?" How do people do this? How do they accept, let it be, flow, go? How do we truly embrace uncertainty or concepts like "we're all trying to do the best we can"[5] or believe that by leaving a situation alone, it will remedy itself? Is there really something like IT that emerges and speaks to us?

Truth, to me, has always been a very tricky word. Mostly, it seems like truth is, more often than not, dependent on one person's perspective. My experiences have led me to believe in certain truths that not only may seem ridiculous to someone else but possibly completely inaccurate or even not applicable. Instead of *truth*, I am coming to feel the word *aha* is possibly more appropriate. I have one aha that feels like truth, but I may have another aha in a few weeks or years that supplants that first aha. It may change what I felt was truth, it may have reinforced it, or it may just tweak it a bit.

This all points to the fact that there is a lot of new learning around ways of being, perceiving, and living. The visual that, ironically, has come to mind as I am tying together all the threads of part one of the *Book of iiwii* is *loose ends*. I hate loose ends. I think this phrase may have an uncomfortable connotation for many of us. Loose ends imply that something hasn't been figured out. It flies in the face of "everything needs to tie together in a nice and neat little package." And this, as I reflect on it, is precisely why it fits so well as a final visual for **iiwii.**

We must accept that there are always going to be loose ends in life, things we need to accept because we literally have no other choice. There are times when nothing seems to tie off in a way that completely makes sense. Accepting loose ends as part of life, like all the other concepts and stories presented so far, is yet another one of our tools for times when we want, need, and/or have no choice but to do an **iiwii.**

Transformation, like the creation of a pearl, happens in infinitesimally small ways. It is much more nuanced than simply shifting from a *doing* to a *being* mode. Most of us at this point have heard the statement made famous by, among others, the Dalai Lama: that we need to remember we are human *beings* first and foremost, not human *doings.*

Whether we are moving slowly or standing still, we can perhaps gently challenge ourselves to look at the world from different directions and different points of view, in the same way a field of sunflowers faces and follows the arc of the sun. The movement is imperceptible. The shift, however, at the end of the day is dramatic.

In conclusion, **iiwii.** is not concerned with mapping out a destination. It is all about just knowing, getting our bearings about where we are right now. It can feel like rooting, letting ourselves bloom a bit where we've been planted. As well, it can feel like being stuck and even being momentarily frozen stiff:

> **And now:** I'm in a cave with small children and having a panic attack. Snap out of it. Unfreeze. Drip, drip. I've got this. We've got this. Accept and let it be, get oriented to the surroundings, and then get out, fast!

It means cultivating the *serenity* that becomes the byproduct of **iiwii.** We embrace a call to rest, which often can be the reset, refresh, and replenishment we need. We pause and do nothing. We get quiet, hearing what is asking to be heard:

> **Not now:** we slow down and stop the frenetic activity. That allows us then to hear the absurd inner voice that says, "Take Herman into Joanie's room. And yes, he will fit through the doors." Do nothing and let things flow, even if they are tears of emotion.

iiwii. suggests we move away from a stance of right and wrong. We say the prayer, make the request, and get comfortable with not always knowing. We feel into our next step if, indeed, there is even a step that needs to be taken at all right now. There is a remarkable book entitled *Emergent Strategy,* which beautifully aligns with the **iiwii.** approach to taking things in the slow spirit of quiet emergence. In it, author adrienne maree brown brilliantly offers this true pearl of wisdom: "How we are at the small scale is how we are at the large scale. . . . Transform yourself to transform the world."[6]

> **For now:** we start exactly where we are and let go of definition and naming. Don't get hung up on understanding life; focus more on just living it. Be open to a both/and approach. We are both

related and not related to these precious and beloved cousins of ours who live in England. We can both survive death threats and be scared at the same time. A pearl can be both gritty and lovely. An aha can be both the truth and just the first of many more ahas. Embrace the mystery and let it go.

THE FLIPPING POINT

And now, to turn all this upside down,
please flip over this book for Part Two.

Note: Flip past the first few blank pages to reach the start of Part Two.

Taking an **iiwii.** break at Equinimity Tucson

We stand in the middle of the quiet and let stillness find us.

iiwii.

ENDNOTES

CHAPTER ONE

1 The actual quote is "Let life happen to you. Believe me: life is in the right, in any case." Rainer Maria Rilke, *Letters to a Young Poet*, trans. M. D. Herter Norton (New York: W. W. Norton, 1954), 55. Several other translations (*Letter 9*) use the word "always."

2 William Safire, "It Is What It Is: Using Tautophrases to Duck and Deflect," *Taipei Times* (March 5, 2006): https://www.taipeitimes.com/News/editorials/archives/2006/03/05/2003295843.

3 Safire, "It Is What It Is."

4 Douglas McCollam, "It Is What It Is . . . But What Is It?" Slate (February 15, 2006): https://slate.com/culture/2008/02/it-is-what-it-is-a-sports-cliche-for-our-times.html.

5 "It is what it is," *Urban Dictionary*, https://www.urbandictionary.com/define.php?term=It%20is%20what%20it%20is.

6 McCollam, "It Is What It Is."

CHAPTER TWO

1 "Katherine Mansfield," *Wikipedia* (updated November 18, 2022): https://en.wikipedia.org/wiki/Katherine_Mansfield.

2 Helen Simpson, "The Outsider: Why Katherine Mansfield Still Divides Opinion 100 Years after Her Death," *The Guardian*, January 7, 2023, https://www.theguardian.com/books/2023/jan/07/the-outsider-why-katherine-mansfield-divided-opinion.

3 Anne Walther, "What Is Wabi Sabi? The Elusive Beauty of Imperfection," *Japan Objects* (January 8, 2021): https://japanobjects.com/features/wabi-sabi.

4 Equinimity is a Tucson-based nonprofit incorporating Equine-Assisted Somatic Experiencing (EASE™) techniques through the support and presence of their herd of six magnificent horses (Little Man, Epona, Freedom, Blue, Brown, and Ralph). To learn more, visit www.equinimitytucson.com.

5 Austin Bryant, "All about Boro—The Story of Japanese Patchwork: Japanese Upcycle: The Art of Boro," *Heddel* (August 31, 2015): https://www.heddels.com/2015/08/all-about-boro-story-japanese-patchwork/.

6 Noriko Sugano is a resident of Tokyo and greatly insightful to Japanese culture and art. She is a close friend of my dear friend Li-Lin English, who describes her as "a teacher, quilter, finder of lost things, and Japan national tour guide." After asking Noriko about this concept, she shared that she had not heard of it, and it is not widely known in mainstream Japanese culture—unlike, for example, wabi-sabi. Upon graciously researching it, she informed me that the correct pronunciation would be "uketamow" (not "uketamo"), which comes from a dialect of Shounai District in Yamagata prefecture. In standard Japanese, it would be "uketamawaru." See https://www.tsuruokacity.com.

7   Donny Kimball, "Uketamo (I Accept)--Training with the Dewa Sanzan Yamabushi." *A Different Side of Japan* (November 15, 2019): https://donnykimball.com/yamabushi-dewa-sanzan-f724a057d7a4.

8   Charlotte Grysolle, "5 Japanese Life Philosophies Worth Knowing" (May 6, 2022): https://www.charlottegrysolle.com/5-japanese-life-philosophies-worth-knowing/.

CHAPTER THREE

1   Martha Beck, *The Joy Diet* (New York: Crown, 2003): 9.

2   Nisha Moodley, "Procrastination vs. Percolation (and How to Tell the Difference)," *Nisha Moodley,* (August 24, 2012): https://nishamoodley.com/procrastination-vs-percolation/.

3   Catherine Meeks, *Night Is Long but Light Comes in the Morning: Meditations for Racial Healing* (Harrisburg, PA: Morehouse, 2022).

4   Tricia Hersey, *Rest Is Resistance: A Manifesto* (New York: Little, Brown Spark, 2022). Tricia Hersey is founder of the Nap Ministry.

5   "Log Jam," *Google Dictionary,* https://www.google.com/search?q=definition+of++log-jam.

6   "Logjam," *Merriam-Webster Dictionary,* https://www.merriam-webster.com/dictionary/logjam.

7   "Log-Jam," *Collins English Dictionary,* https://www.collinsdictionary.com/us/dictionary/english/log-jam.

8   Yongey Mingyur Rinpoche with Eric Swanson, *Joyful Wisdom: Embracing Change and Finding Freedom* (New York: Three Rivers, 2009).

9   Emerging Technology from the ArXiv, "Logjams Aren't Really Jammed at All, Say Geoscientists," *MIT Technology Review* (November 19, 2019): www.technologyreview.com/2019/11/19/131899/logjams-arent-really-jammed-at-all-say-geoscientists/. The key quote was: "The first study of the way logs got pinned in rivers reveals that those seemingly trapped in a logjam move steadily, if slowly, downriver."

10 Barbara L. Fredrickson, *Positivity: Discover the Upward Spiral That Will Change Your Life* (New York: Harmony, 2009), 42.

11 As cited in Soon Teo, "Do Nothing in Order to Do More," *Tao in You* (November 2, 2015): https://tao-in-you.com/do-nothing-in-order-to-do-more/.

CHAPTER FOUR

1   "Welcome to Firle: A Country Estate in the South Downs National Park," Firle, https://firle.com/estate-villages/.

2   "The Gage Family," Firle, https://firle.com/house-visits/the-family/.

3   Lisa Rodriguez, "80 Years Post-Pendergast, Kansas City Mayoral Hopefuls Wonder If Local Control of Police Is Worth It," *NPR/KCUR Politics Elections and Government,* March 29, 2019, https://www.kcur.org/politics-elections-and-government/2019-03-29/80-years-post-pendergast-kansas-city-mayoral-hopefuls-wonder-if-local-control-of-police-is-worth-it.

4   Albert Einstein, *Living Philosophies* (New York: Simon & Schuster, 1931), 6.

5   Scott Smith, "Psychology: A Sense of Mystery May Be the Spice of Life," *Capital Gazette* (February 6, 2014): https://www.capitalgazette.com/cg2-arc-140206cl-smith-20140206-story.html.

6   Smith, "Psychology: A Sense of Mystery."

CHAPTER FIVE

1 Oliver Burkeman, *Four Thousand Weeks: Time Management for Mortals* (New York: Farrar, Straus and Giroux, 2021), 137, 139.

2 Ouwtre Tlievna, *The Simple Essence of Life* (Scotts Valley, CA: CreateSpace, 2021).

3 As a US Senate staffer, I was privileged to meet Senate Chaplain Richard Halverson. This was one of his Bible study illustrations.

4 Peter Wood, "Liminal Space," undated handout.

5 Byron Katie, *A Thousand Names for Joy: Living in Harmony with the Way Things Are* (New York: Three Rivers, 2007), 55.

6 adrienne maree brown, *Emergent Strategy: Shaping Change, Changing Worlds* (Chico, CA: AK Press, 2017), 52–53.

Printed in the USA
CPSIA information can be obtained
at www.ICGtesting.com
LVHW090233091024
793326LV00002B/218

BOOK OF

iiwii

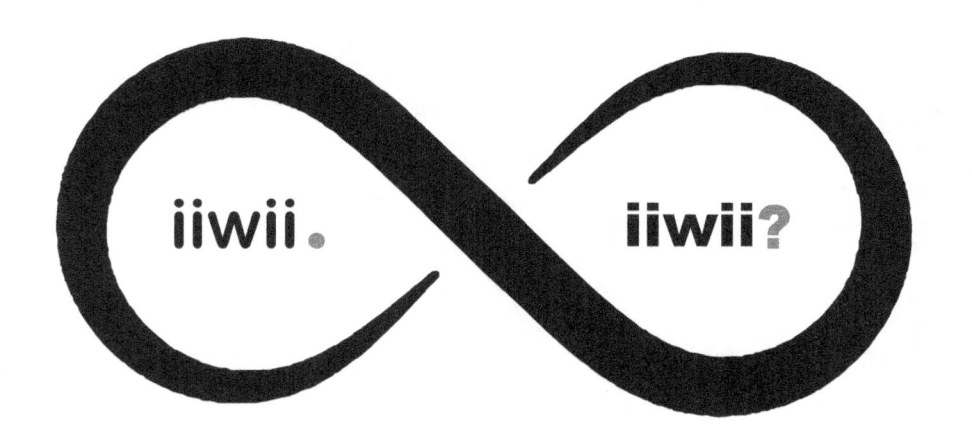

it is what it is.

iiwii.   iiwii?

is it what it is?

KATHY LEWIS SAWYER

PART TWO

is it what it is?

iiwii → *pronounced:* /ēwē/

iiwii?

CONTENTS

6

The Origin Story II

The best way out is always through.

—Robert Frost
(American poet, 1874–1963)

This *Book of iiwii* has undergone a much longer germination period than I thought it would. And yet, as our friend Mr. Frost reminds us above, sometimes there are no shortcuts. The best way out is right through the muddle and the mess. In Origin Story I, I shared the process and origin of how all the random ideas came together to create the book I knew I needed to read. It focused mainly on a surprising number of aha moments that stemmed from the obnoxious phrase *it is what it is* that had highjacked my brain at the time. All I wanted to do at that point was just to start getting all this **iiwii** stuff down on paper in some mildly coherent way and be done with it.

Ha. We make plans and the gods laugh, right? What emerged was that Inner Truth (IT) voice I was learning how to cultivate through my ever-growing practice of being still. The message was simply this: "You are not done." IT let me know there was something distinctively amiss in **iiwii.** and my life-is-always-in-the-right theory of acceptance.

Somehow I just needed to keep letting the book unfold. The logjam of this book's message was starting ever so slowly to loosen as I just let things flow. Once again, I became plagued with an irksome, albeit much cuter, phrase that emerged to kick off this Origin Story II—what would become part two of the book. It was *just keep swimming.* For those who might

be unfamiliar with it, this three-word piece of wisdom is espoused over and over by an endearing, short-term memory-suffering blue tang fish in *Finding Nemo*. And so, aligning myself with her philosophy, like Dory, I kept swimming as I waited to see what happened next.

I had decided to take a solo trip across country to focus on my writing and to "do some research." My destination was North Carolina and I happened to be right on the shores of its breathtaking Outer Banks. I remember sitting by a window, looking out at the Atlantic Ocean in a post-sunset serenity afterglow, which is how the image of Dory had naturally come to mind. Here is what I wrote in my handy companion journal that, as we know, always travels with me:

While I am thrilled beyond words to be at the ocean, I am sitting in an air-conditioned room with a very large picture window facing the ocean, so I don't have to go out and sweat in the 500% humidity. I went for a walk earlier, and there were not one but thousands, actually millions, of slimy jellyfish everywhere, in the water and on the sand where people are supposed to stroll, right next to the water.

A friendly North Carolina family shared that they had never ever, in "all our time of coming here, seen the jellyfish like this." The dad said, "And these are the red ones. If they sting ya, it hurts like a son of a you know what, and then you have to pry the tentacles out. Our daughter here stepped on one just this morning [daughter tears up on cue]. Yep, you wanna stay away from them."

His wife then finished by saying, "Well, at least it's keepin' people out of the water. There were three sharks just right out there yesterday, and we all saw them, fins and all, sticking right out of the waves"—pointing to someplace way too close, even though at this point I wasn't even looking and was preparing to hightail it back to my room as fast as I could. I smiled with an odd look that likely said, "Yikes, thanks, but I gotta get outta here right now." They understood.

As I am pulled for some reason to share this story, I realize there is a side of me that sometimes likes to complain—just a bit. Sometimes more than a bit. Instead of the gorgeous sunset, I focused on the jellyfish explosion. Instead of losing myself in the ecstasy of the ocean waves, especially since I am a desert dweller who loves water, I am looking for the telltale triangle topsides of sharks roaming around. I am thinking about sweat when I should be thinking about the fact that I am away, alone, by myself, and giddy to be able to have carved out this time from my busy schedule.

Instead of focusing on asking the cute family who has been coming here for years for one or two recommendations of, perhaps, a nice ocean-front restaurant, I get into a conversation about prying red slimy tentacles out of their poor daughter's feet. See what I mean?

I am not proud of the fact that I am a closet complainer. I try to hide it as much as possible. The truth is, it is there and always has been. I remember back to my high-school days and being aware of this very unadmirable trait even then. Once, one of my best friends and I even decided we would create a "no complain day" just to see if we could do it. Neither of us made it to lunch, and I am fairly certain I caved by the second hour. I know I went down first.

What is the relevance of including this particular entry? Part two of the *Book of iiwii* emerged to address what I came to realize was missing from part one. It takes the **iiwii.** concepts of letting things be, flow, or go and turns them upside down by asking some questions:

What about the things that we legitimately cannot accept?

What about the importance of questioning, of not settling for the status quo?

Could there be an opposite to **iiwii.**?

As we dive into Origin Story II, which will attempt to address some of these weighty concepts, it occurred to me (in an **iiwii.** post-percolation aha moment) that an unusual but oddly appropriate place to begin might be with our very human urge to complain.

Complaining is underrated. It truly is a sleuth form of resisting "what is" and wanting it to be different. It smacks of nonacceptance. We often

ascribe a negative quality to it, and admittedly, it can—and often does—mean absolutely nothing other than that we are grouchy, hangry, or tired. That said, it can also mean something more—and ultimately more positive. It can be an indicator that we may want to rethink something, reroute, and plug in a slightly different destination—for the moment, the day, or a timeframe substantially longer. It becomes an early warning system that maybe something is off track. It nudges us toward thinking about a change in what we're doing to possibly achieve a better outcome.

From part one, you know that I am a big fan of Eckhart Tolle. In his iconic book, *The Power of Now*, he states, "To complain is always nonacceptance of what is. It invariably carries an unconscious negative charge. When you complain, you make yourself into a victim. When you speak out, you are in your power. So, change the situation by taking action or by speaking out if necessary or possible; leave the situation or accept it. All else is madness."[1]

When I read this, it was an epiphany for me. First, as mentioned, I saw complaining in a slightly different light—not necessarily as turning ourselves into a victim but more like what can happen when we take a "wrong" turn, or are about to do so and we suddenly have an early warning feeling that something is amiss. As our internal GPS is frantically starting to reroute us, we have three distinct choices. In keeping with the GPS metaphor, they are:

1. Accept the situation. Enjoy the ride and just keep going the way we are going.

2. Change the situation. Do the reroute and acknowledge that it may require needing to backtrack and probably will take more time. We acknowledge there may be a better path to our destination than we had originally thought.

3. Leave the situation now. Pull over, get out, and just walk. Or, alternatively, plug in a whole new destination completely different from where we were originally going and make a dramatic shift. It may not be permanent, but for now, it is imperative. We

pull together data and gradually see if this new direction feels right and is proving to be a better option.

The notion of choosing to accept, change, or leave a situation was a major breakthrough, giving me a beautifully simple 1-2-3 checklist for what I knew was something very *not simple* to execute. Of course, I turned it into an acronym—ACL: accept, change, or leave.

Accept is textbook **iiwii.** mode from part one. Ditching the "I should have known better," we go with the new flow, like the mass of jumbled logs, and see where we land. We accept our situation, at least for now, exactly the way life has handed it to us in this moment.

Items two and three, change and leave the situation, are foundational to the **iiwii?** philosophy of part two. Here, it will be all about change, redirection, and often achieving something that is of breakthrough nature—even, or especially, if it is just for us.

ENOUGH IS ENOUGH—DO IT OR DON'T

Getting this **iiwii** project started in earnest was more than I had bargained for. I had accepted that writing this book was a reality. Sheer force of will had taken over, plus I hired a writing coach. It was official, right? The first year came and went. The second year came and went with nothing to show for it except a growing tab with Shirin, my coach, who lovingly started to press me a bit with observations like "I'm OK with getting paid, but I don't really feel like I'm earning it since you haven't really written anything yet." Ouch. It wasn't totally true; I had my outline done, plus some ideas for stories, selected theories to support my themes, and tons of quotes already lined up. That wasn't nothing.

In year three, reality started to sink in: for the life of me, I really could not get the first chapter finished. The draft chapter that I had written years earlier that I loved and that had been erased by my iPad still haunted me whenever I sat down to get going. Classic resistance and resignation set in.

Before the truth sets you free, it tends to make you miserable.

—Richard Rohr, *Falling Upward: A Spirituality for the Two Halves of Life*
(American Franciscan friar and writer on spirituality
based in Albuquerque, New Mexico)

I realized I either had to scrap this idea—accepting that I no longer really intended to write this *Book of iiwii*, lest I go crazy with beating myself up over this whole thing and cut the book dream loose, *or* I had to change my approach—dramatically.

Something needed to change. What did I do? I followed my own **iiwii.** advice: I tuned in to how I was feeling, I tuned out all the mental chatter, and I waited for the embedded, reluctant aha message to emerge. What was IT saying? Quietly, I began to hear my Inner Truth come forward. It came not as an answer but as a simple question: "How?"

How do I make myself accountable for something I really did not need to do or was being asked or expected to do by someone else? I have always been mindful of deadlines—at least those externally created and enforced. Whether it is ego, pride, or a desire not to let myself or others down, I usually always find a way to get something done if there is a deadline, even if it is in the eleventh hour. So how do I do *this*—something that requires internal motivation, something just for myself—when no one is telling me I have to do it?

As if to address this very question, one day Shirin asked me something that hit like a dense adobe brick. Sensing my growing frustration, she said, "Kathy, can you respect yourself enough to give yourself time to write?" I recall gritting my teeth, ready to jump into a whole list of reasons around why my life was too busy to be able to do this right now. And yet, she was exactly right. I was so caught up in the business of everything else that I had totally forgotten the business of myself. And not simply my general state of well-being. This was more about my passionate self, my *vibrant* self.

It's so easy, for women especially, but really for all of us at times, to try to be the keepers of *what is*—and to maintain that *what is* for everyone around us. Once again, I call forth Anne Lamott's quote about lighthouses. It bears repeating: "Lighthouses don't go running all over an island looking for boats to save; they just stand there shining."[2] Instead of running all around our respective "islands" in doing mode, possibly savior mode and definitely overwhelm mode, Lamott reminds us to remember something. What is our real job?? Are we focusing our energy in a way that our efforts are effective—*not* for everyone else, but for ourselves?

As a sidenote, I love lighthouses. Maybe this is one reason this quote speaks so strongly to me and I used it in part one. As I was pondering whether a lighthouse could possibly also be a good analogy for part two, I had a well-timed discovery. I came across a fascinating article on lighthouses in an online magazine, titled *How Things Work*. The article and even its title were spot on for what I wanted to find out: "Inside a Lighthouse: Discover the Tried-and-Tested Technology Behind These Maritime Navigational Beacons."

What hit me as I read about all that goes into making a lighthouse work was that even though it appears to be doing very little, other than standing there shining, it is actually in full blown action mode. Housing and harnessing massive amounts of energy and intricate systems of lamps and lenses, it has all sorts of things going on beyond what is visible, beyond what appears to be some simply focused beams. If you are a lighthouse lover, here are the details:

> At the top of a lighthouse is a large, rotating light. Instead of scattering the light in all directions, light exits the beacon in a single beam. The lens placed in front of the lamp has stepped sections that focus the light into the centre…The focused light is better able to penetrate the dark, and rotating the light means it's visible to sailors approaching from all directions. This powerful beam can even cut through fog for maximum effectiveness.[3]

For me, this description provides a beautiful visual, a template. It is by getting ourselves pulled together and focused, doing the "real" job of first finding our own inner vibrancy, that we are then able to provide a higher beam for everyone around us. The key here is doing it first of all for ourselves, then if other boats (or people) in our respective oceans benefit as well, all the better. So, back to my journey on how to get started. I realized I had to come to terms with being stuck, stop distracting myself by scattering energy all over the place and get beyond that uncomfortable place we explored in the "Do Nothing" section in part one.

As they say, the right teacher shows up at the right time. Her name was Josie and she is wise beyond her years. It was during this pre-launch time,

she and I had a pivotal conversation. She suggested that it seemed like I might be "out of alignment." What I *wanted* to do was not aligned with what I actually *was* doing. "At least," I confessed to her, "I am in alignment with the *need* for realignment" trying to be funny in a not-at-all funny way.

And yet, she had helped me nail it. Being out of alignment was the quandary and yet, this realization and being able to name it, unexpectedly became my starting point. No longer a want, or a should, it became elevated to a different plane—it was a *need*. I needed to take action and harness my energy. It was time to become that shining lighthouse and *do something* to get myself focused.

SO. No more excuses. It was March, and I created a deadline: December 31 of that same year, the first draft would be complete.

How does this all tie in to **it is what it is**? In finally making this monumental choice to create a timeline, I put into play part of the ACL acronym. I did a true **iiwii?** and took actions that initiated for my situation both a change and a leave. I changed the way I had been approaching the book and actualized an absolute deadline—to myself, for myself—that needed to be named. Additionally, to get it all started, I realized I actually needed to leave my environment and daily routines. I needed to experience, even for a bit, a complete change of scenery so that all those very creative excuses and strategies for distraction that I endlessly provided for myself would hopefully be removed.

And so I did something dramatic. I had no idea if it would work. I requested a one-month sabbatical from work, which admittedly is not remotely in the realm of possibility for many. I honestly didn't think it was remotely in my realm either—until I asked. I was equal parts amazed and shocked when the two founders of the nonprofit I worked for said, "Yes, go get that book started. We will be here and will reach out if we need anything."

BIRTH OF **iiwii?**

My focus up until then had been only on the **iiwii.** side of things, figuring out ways of working within the confines of a given situation or system,

whatever "system" it was that I found myself in—like a cave. Accept, take things in, reorient, embrace the uncertainty. Do what you can with what you've got and let things be, flow, and go, dammit.

Then came the point when it finally hit me: I realized that I only had half a book. Maybe, I thought, this was why getting started was tough— because the whole picture hadn't emerged yet. While I thought I had done my due diligence and gathered all appropriate data, outline ready to go, pen poised in hand, it hit me: there was an entirely different concept I needed to address.

And this is when all those weighty questions started forming a line, right inside my ever-expanding brain. What about not settling for the status quo? What about the importance of taking a stand, of being authentic to ourselves, and doing something that needs to be done? Is there a time when we must accept we can no longer accept something the way it is? *Is it what it is?* Could that be just as true? My conclusion was yes, it could be just as true, and yet did I really want to do a whole second part of this book? Before I could even answer that last and very key question, IT, my Inner Truth friend from **iiwii.**, weighed in: "Yes, it's happening."

OK, I agreed, but my vision was to keep it all as simple as possible. Why not just flip the **iiwii.** concepts from part one on their heads? The theme of acceptance flips to the theme of questioning: How do we learn how to question whether a situation is right or wrong versus just standing there and accepting it? I will share an experience that happened for me at a very young age, when this skill got a jumpstart while taking a stroll with my mother in a forest one day.

Do nothing, of course, becomes do something. Instead of a call to rest, it is a call to action. Instead of the lovely **iiwii.** mode encouraging us to slow down, be still, and allow ourselves to be in a place to experience serenity, again we do the opposite. In the equally lovely yet different mode of **iiwii?**, we get going, become curious, and find the joy in getting things done. I will share a personal achievement of my own—which was both highly unusual and utterly out of character—that happened one recent winter in my backyard.

Embrace mystery, the third theme of part one, was a bit trickier. How would I flip this concept over? To refresh, it tells the story of our "cousins" of Firle Place and being open to something that required a leap of faith, an open heart, and the relinquishing of control and the need for proof.

The answer emerged immediately. Of course! What was the opposite of embracing the unknown? Eliminating mystery and uncertainty. Exactly what Marjorie had wanted: proof, data, control. This was right in my lineage wheelhouse. We create checklists, formulas, and processes. We study variables and draw conclusions gained by trial and error that then support reliable procedures that can be replicated sustainably into the future. Yes, this felt like the opposite of embracing mystery. Map out a system, a blueprint, then build it. And I immediately knew exactly which story I needed to tell to smack this one right out of the *Book of iiwii* ballpark: the one about my grandmother's "crazy" neighbors.

And so part two was ready. It all started coming together. I had found the missing piece in realizing that *is it what it is?* made just as much sense and was just as important a concept as *it is what it is.* Not only that, but, happily, I further noted that, as an acronym, it also had the exact same letters—**iiwii.** Double bonus. And, like **iiwii.**, I decided it, too, will have its own unique font throughout the book—just for easier reading: **iiwii?** As a woman of great wisdom once revealed:

> ### *A truth may resemble its opposite.*
> —Oracle of Delphi

The situations are endless and often complex, but the question is simpler than we think: When do we need to accept that we can no longer accept something the way it is? When is enough, enough? It was finally time to get this book finished, and I decided to follow my own advice. I had reached the tipping point, which I decided to call the flipping point. I could no longer accept this book not getting done, and so I flipped **iiwii.** upside down and got going. The call to action had begun.

7

Insight #1: Question

Remember to look up at the stars, not down at your feet.
Try to make sense of what you are and wonder about what
makes the universe exist. Be curious.

—Stephen Hawking
(English theoretical physicist, cosmologist, and author, 1942–2018)

Oh, Mother . . . Bears!

It is amazing how much we learn by osmosis: no words exchanged, just taking it in. One of my earliest memories took place in a forest in Minnesota. I was about seven, and our family had driven up to Lake Vermilion, one of the ten thousand lakes that were advertised on the state's license plate. I knew this because the whole drive up from Missouri we played the license-plate game, and I was just learning to read, so I was avidly reading the full text on every single plate we saw. I was very excited that we would be staying at one of these lakes.

Once we got there and all settled in, my two older siblings raced off somewhere, and I was stuck alone with my mom. In a very uncharacteristic move, she asked if I would like to take a walk with her in the forest behind our little cabin, to which I ecstatically agreed.

My mom was always different from other moms I knew. While most of my friends' mothers were typically coiffed and well turned out, my mom was usually a bit disheveled with zero thought put into what clothing might land on her body on any given day. She almost always had a cigarette in

one hand and often a camera—a large one—in the other. If it was after 5:00 p.m., the camera was replaced with a stiff gin martini.

Driving cross country was fun and effortless for her, so trips like the one to Minnesota happened often in my childhood. In fact, she enjoyed her open-highway adventures so much that once CB (citizen band) radios were invented, she immediately got one and gave herself the handle (nickname) Silver Fox. It humorously was not referring to her (graying hair) self but to her beloved car at the time, a silver Electra 225, affectionately called the Deuce and a Quarter. She loved gadgets, so the CB radio, a pre-cellphone form of on-the-road communication, was no doubt nirvana for her.

All of this is to say, even way back then, my mother was the epitome of someone who truly enjoyed what we would now call "doing her own thing." So when the invitation to take a stroll down a forest path was made, I snatched it.

I was little, the size of an Oz munchkin with small legs that made it a bit tricky to keep up with her, which was not really a problem because she was slow. Back then, I do not think the concept of jogging had even been created. I never saw her on a bicycle. I'm not even sure if she knew how to ride one. While apparently she was very athletic as a younger woman, by the time she had all of us, she was not.

What she was, however, was someone who loved being out in nature. We both did. What she also was, was someone who always took the time, or at least tried, to answer the many questions that, even as a young girl, I remember always asking. Stephen Hawking had my number down pat when in the quote leading us into this chapter he encourages us to look at the stars and let ourselves wonder and be curious. My curiosity was insatiable.

So we were slowly strolling down this long path with what I remember were very tall trees all around us. We took a few twists and turns and then stopped to catch our breath. Did I mention she smoked quite a bit? While we were standing there, with her admiring the scenery and me kicking dirt around, happy as her ecstatic, made-the-cut explorer sidekick, she suddenly exclaimed, "Look!"

"Where?" I replied, my tiny head swiveling in every direction I could possibly make it swivel but still seeing nothing.

"Over there, by that bush!"

And before my eyes, there was a sight I could not believe we had the *incredible luck* to see: a great big brown bear and two little, tiny cubs! I was immediately awestruck. I absolutely loved animals as a little kid, and this was too good to be true. Not one but *two* little adorable bear cubs!

I turned back around to my mom, who had been right behind me, to share the obvious glee and excitement we were both feeling about this moment. Yet as I turned around, I noticed something strange.

She wasn't there.

There are many different types of questions that can present themselves to us during any given day. Some can be instantaneous, part of our natural human wiring to survive. In the case of me, my mother, and the bears in the forest, I still remember it as though I were right there. My question was: Do I stand here and spend some more time watching these adorable, squishy-soft-looking cubs and their mother, who, I noticed happily, was starting to lumber toward me, or do I do what I now see my mother was doing and run like crazy?

Several yards ahead of me, up the path, I saw the rubber-soled bottoms of her sneakerish shoes kicking up dust everywhere, taking her farther and farther away. I had never seen her run before.

Apparently, the primal urge to survive superseded my seven-year-old urge to cuddle a bear cub, and so, I also decided to run with my little legs in full-throttle *go* mode as I followed my mother out of the woods.

The question of what to do was instantaneously answered. And in that moment, without any awareness, a very, very strong fear of bears and forests was infused right into my entire being.

THE *MAYFLOWER*

We are all wired to survive, as my forest experience suggests, but I have also learned that apparently this wiring is especially pronounced in my *particular* ancestral line. As daughters and sons of pioneers, immigrants, and

even *Mayflower* voyagers, we seem to have been a pull-yourself-up-by-the-bootstraps lot. One such ancestor, who ventured across the Atlantic Ocean in 1620 bound for the New World, happened to be a guy named John Howland. His claim to fame is that he was the only passenger who fell off the *Mayflower* into the ocean and survived.[1] As the story goes, it was during a violent storm, and after being tossed over the side of the ship after hitting a huge wave, he somehow "managed to grab hold of a trailing rope, giving the *Mayflower* crew just enough time to rescue him with a boat-hook."

He was none the worse for wear, apparently, as, after arriving on the fertile soil of the New World, he went on to get married and have a very large number of little Howlands, which created—as an aside—an explosive number of descendants who are listed all over Ancestry.com.

In addition to being wired for survival—in my case, really hardwired, thanks to the Howland contribution of courage to our familial thread—it also turns out we are all apparently created to be oblivious to most, if not all, of our inherited internal encoding. This wiring can occur from our personal experiences or, as revealed through the growing field of epigenetics, from experiences of ancestors we never even knew but with whom we become inextricably intertwined through our DNA lineage.

Many of these imprints of fear—mother bear . . . run!—biases, or even deeply buried traumas can simply become just part of who we are, part of the ancestral water we swim in, so to speak, all the time. This is why, for me, in thinking about **iiwii? is it what it is?**, there is a prerequisite, an intention for unlearning, that needs to take place.

This unlearning can happen by simply taking the time to notice with fresh eyes or opened ears some of the age-old patterns we've become conditioned to overlook.

These can range from deep-seated, unexplainable fears and biases to outdated hand-me-down expressions to which we hardly give a second thought. One of these tumbled out of my mouth recently, probably one time out of hundreds or more that I have used this phrase and never even batted an eye: "Let's kill two birds with one stone." Today, it has become a quirky catch-all phrase meaning something like: "Let's go to the movies *and* eat a dinner of popcorn."

Since most of us no longer have to hunt and kill birds for our evening meal, the expression's relevancy is long past. For the bird lovers among us, it is an outworn phrase that probably merits ditching or replacing. ("Kill two mosquitos with one swat," perhaps?) The point is, like many things, we probably never even think about it or even notice our use of it since it has become, for centuries, such an ingrained expression. Unlearning happens as we start to create a habit of not just looking but of truly seeing what's in front of us.

> ***Learn from yesterday, live for today, hope for tomorrow.***
> ***The important thing is not to stop questioning.***
> —Albert Einstein
> (German mathematician and physicist, 1879–1955)

Knowing how and when to ask questions is an art. It is what sets the stage for knowing when a situation is no longer acceptable. In a situation causing a visceral fight, flight, or freeze survival-stress response, we find that we have no choice but to ask and answer a question right in the moment. In my case, during my forest bear encounter, it was: "Do I stay and play (and probably die), or do I bolt and catch up with my mother (and probably live to enjoy the famous Lake Vermilion blueberry pie later that night)?"

The questioning occurs so fast we don't even know we have, in that blink of an eye, asked and answered a question. In doing this, though, quite often there can be some subtle internal rewiring going on as a result of the jarring incident. For years, I was scared of dark forests and large bears. I still did love the idea of bear cubs, however. Even deeper in the impressionable fibers of a young seven-year-old's being, there probably were some other types of inner encoding going on, like, when push comes to shove, as great as moms can be, you ultimately have to rely on yourself to get out of a sticky situation.

On the darker side, some might say it could have fostered feelings of abandonment (victim mentality), and yet, on the lighter side, my preference is to see it, in a weird way, as having engendered feelings of empowerment. I wasn't being dragged, picked up, and whisked away, not having

any clue why I was being taken away from these two roly-poly cubs. In the parlance of today, I got to have agency in my exodus.

Years later, I realized that situation truly had etched itself into me, sort of like a life tattoo. That's why I still have such a vivid memory of the experience. It helped me realize both the subtlety and necessity of well-timed questioning, whether it is in the moment of a threatening situation (do I stay or bolt?) or in the sudden waking up and noticing the incongruence or inappropriateness of a long-used phrase that we never thought to question.

Through experiences, expressions, and ancestral contributions to the many ways we are wired as individuals and as the collective human community, we truly can be blind to the biases ingrained in every single one of us. This is where the unlearning piece especially comes to light. Unlearning can be just as important as learning.

It's so easy to be oblivious because these biases, quite often, are simply the water we swim in, what we are so used to—so much so that we do not even see them. It would be like throwing a farm pond catfish into the salty ocean or Dory into a freshwater (unsalted) farm pond. The water looks exactly the same, at least to the untrained eye. Both look clear, even though the invisible chemistry of each is vastly different. It is the same way a city sidewalk looks just like any other city sidewalk, and yet the experience of walking down some sidewalks can be vastly different depending on our pond, ocean, or other pool of origin. Invisible chemistries exist everywhere, on both sea and land.

The reason I was drawn to highlight catfish is because they were a big part of my "pool" or place of origin. I grew up around farm lakes and ponds, and the catfish was the elusive fish I was always on the quest to catch as a girl with my tiny Zebco fishing rod. I finally did make the catch. As fate would have it, it truly was the one that got away, taking my broken rod, reel, and zest for fishing away with it.

We are each the byproducts of our experiences. Each of us embodies to some extent our ancestral lines. The ponds or oceans that we either flourished or floundered in are what make us who we are. Our filters and biases become the water we swim in, so much so that we don't even notice

them, much less think to question them. Instead of just saying "It is what it is," this is the exact time to flip that expression over and ask, "Is it what it is?"

Lyrics to "You've Got to Be Carefully Taught" from South Pacific

—Oscar Hammerstein II
(German-born American lyricist, 1895–1960)

As editing was deep underway for the *Book of iiwii*, along with hundreds of other things, I learned that we cannot directly quote lyrics from a song unless permission (usually with a hefty fee associated) is obtained. The reference above is to a controversial song from one of the most popular Broadway musicals of the 20th century, released in 1949, *South Pacific*. The lyrics in their entirety are well worth reading but in essence the song underscores how most of us have learned certain views and behaviors from very young ages toward other people and cultures—views that often no longer serve. *South Pacific*, written by Richard Rodgers, with lyrics by Oscar Hammerstein II was noted for its pointedness, unusual for those times, and apparently caused quite a stir.

> "You've Got to Be Carefully Taught" is the least melodic and least musically memorable number from the brilliant score. However, it is the very heart of what Hammerstein is trying to say. Racism, he argues, is a learned behavior, often starting at very early ages. The song caused great controversy. Hammerstein refused all requests to remove the song. It was his show and his message. He and Rodgers were always proud of the song, the show, and the opportunity to open the eyes of audiences to the scourge of prejudice.[2]

At our core, as the full lyrics to this song so boldly express, mindsets of fear, threat, and hatred are indelibly written into our brains at very young ages. Most of us remain unaware of much of this for our entire lives. There are obviously biases toward positive, noteworthy, and lovely elements handed down and worked into our wiring as well, and yet, for our purposes here, we are focusing on the harder stuff, on trying to tease

out and become aware of the invisible imprints that may be hindering us, as opposed to helping us, on our respective life journeys.

Robert M. Sapolsky, author of the book with one of my all-time favorite titles, *Why Zebras Don't Get Ulcers,* captures in very technical terms what happens when we cross paths later with some of the "subjects" of these early childhood or intergenerational "teachings" around who is dangerous and who is not. He states, "Brains distinguish between an Us and a Them in a fraction of a second. Subliminal processing of a Them activates the amygdala and insular cortex, brain regions that are all about fear, anxiety, aggression, and disgust."[3]

In another equally compelling read, *Talking to Strangers* by Malcolm Gladwell,[4] all of this starts to come together in terms of why certain people and/or situations cause very visceral reactions that those involved, especially the perpetrators or initiators, are often clueless to understand. They cannot understand what is compelling them to bypass reason, or comprehend that they even *are* bypassing reason, and push into, in some cases, highly irrational behavior.

Invisible forces exist, like salt in the water, that allow some of us to thrive and others to die, whether emotionally or physically. When we don't feel understood, seen, safe, or that we are swimming in the "right waters," it can be profoundly unsettling. In some cases, it can be lethal.

CAGED BIRD

I have discussed different ways of asking questions from situations of survival ("do I run or stay?") to situations when there was a sudden awakening, pointing to "Could there be a better way?" The last type of questioning I will discuss expands on the latter. It also brings into the storytelling fold our third child, Hannah, who happily arrived on the scene a few years after the Colossal Cave cluster. It must speak to some of that John Howland epigenetic resilience that I made it through that cave ordeal and then willingly went on to have another offspring.

Getting to watch Hannah grow up was fascinating. My Velcro child, as I lovingly called her, exhibited a curious tendency I remember having as a small person too. Through some kind of DNA amplification process

for not-great traits, she and I got the short end of the stick on what I will just call *attachment management,* managing our strong need to be attached at all times to other humans. I secretly called it my "keep the door open" gene. For me, it had not necessarily been a fear of being alone but more of being cut off and disconnected from others. As a toddler, whenever I went outside, even in frigid weather, I used to insist that the back door stay open. The same applied to my bedroom door at night. As I got older, I always made sure I knew how to lock and unlock doors so I would not be shut out. For me, it was an open-door world or bust.

I had this predisposition (a.k.a. quirk) despite living in the *same* house all my growing-up years. One would think I would feel secure enough not to constantly need access to or a visual of those around me—not to constantly need proof that they were all still there and hadn't disturbingly disappeared in a puff of smoke or run out of the forest when I wasn't looking.

For Hannah, it did not help that we made two huge moves during the early, formative years for all three of the kids. And yet, in a strange way, as I am reflecting on all this, *maybe* it did help. She found herself so far out of her comfort zone that she had no option but to eventually create some strategies to deal with the fear of being separated or detached from that which made her feel secure. When we made the second move, the Velcro tendency definitely got worse before it got better, which seems to be a consistent life lesson for many things.

What Hannah received on the positive side of the ancestral DNA ledger was and continues to be remarkable. Among many other things, she has a power of observation of others and of situations that is second to none. She also has always seemed to me to be incredibly self-aware. That said, sometimes too much self-awareness can be just as tricky as too little. I have memories of witnessing her anxiousness when the thought of standing in front of a class to present something—or just standing there in front of people *at all*—was terrifying for her. She was *too* aware and *too* worried about herself, others, and who knows what else.

This had been true all the way back to preschool but just seemed to keep growing instead of waning as the years trundled by. I remember one occasion vividly when she was in sixth grade and had to recite a Maya

Angelou poem called "Caged Bird."[5] It was a coming-of-age game-changer for her but as referenced above, in a way that got worse before it got better. It is as though the breathtaking words to this extraordinary Angelou poem became a bit like a foreshadowing of things to come or at least the beginning of a possible new trajectory for Hannah. She loved the poem and had practiced and practiced. She went in the day it was her turn to do the poetry reading and seemed confident in a trembling sort of way, not unlike the fearful caged bird she was talking about. Later that day, when she got home, the only thing she said was, "I cried." She does not remember this sequence entirely the same way I do, but since I am writing the story, I am putting it down, with her nod, the way I remember it. What happened next is where this starts to tie in to part two's **iiwii?** concept of questions. And it marked the beginning of an entirely new way of being for Hannah.

After the "Caged Bird" breakdown in front of all her classmates (did I mention she was one of the new kids that year too?), she decided to ask herself a question, a tough one—the kind I referred to earlier that is hardcore for an adult to muster the nerve to ask, much less a shy little sixth-grader. It was: "What do I need to do *not to be* that [scared] girl anymore?"

We have all been there, with hundreds of ways we could ask a version of that same question. And how often have we been able to nail it? To take a square look, head on, at a fundamental part of our wiring, then ask the question honestly and fiercely of ourselves: "Can I do something about this?" This is not easy stuff, and I will add that asking that question is a very, very private thing. It involves only one person: the person doing the asking.

Change didn't happen overnight, and yet in some ways, it felt like it. As sixth grade came to an end, there was a noticeably different demeanor starting to emerge for Hannah. At first, it presented as just a slow, quiet self-confidence, barely perceptible. She seemed to be more relaxed and actually interested in extending herself to make a few more friends. Now, part of this, admittedly, may have just been part of the natural maturation process from elementary school to middle school, but, in my experience, that was a time when things could completely go sideways, often with confidence shrinking, especially for girls, not growing. It was as though, for

quite a while, she had hung back in her "cage," watching it all going on, and then, *bam*, she opened the door herself and decided to fly out of there.

Hannah is now in her late twenties. She has literally flourished beyond words in the years since her Maya Angelou meltdown moment. And yet her question still was not fully answered. Apparently, she shared with me, it had one more iteration to go through.

It went something like this: "Now that I've got a handle on dealing with some of the everyday anxiety and fear stuff, how do I deal with the *big* one, the one that haunts many of us, consciously or not, to our core? It is basically the fear of the ultimate disconnection—of death and dying."

As lighthearted in some ways as my *Book of iiwii* is meant to be, I am finding that some very unexpected elements keep wanting to emerge that are taking us into deeper waters.

A Skull Tattoo

Sometime during pandemic peak (my phrase for the mid-COVID-19 stretch), Hannah, like everyone else in this new remote-work era, came home to get a change of scenery, free food, and wine. And, of course, her real motive, I know, was to have lots of quality time with her mom and dad and dogs, but especially her mom.

OK, not really. That said, it was within just a few minutes of her changing into her sleeveless desert attire that I noticed a tattoo peeking out from under her inner upper arm. I asked to see it, and, I must say, it was an utter mystery to me as to why she chose what she chose. I was a bit blown away by what I saw.

First, it was beautifully done. I am not a tattoo person myself—needles and permanency flip me out—but hers was lovely. It had a very intricate prickly pear cactus next to a perfect rendition of a taller saguaro cactus, and right in the middle of both was the shocker: a skull of a dead cow or bull with horns. I understood the significance of the cacti: Hannah had fallen head over heels for succulents, thanks to our dear friend Raul, and gradually that love spread to the spinier desert dwellers—majestic saguaros and the stunning prickly pears. But the skull? I had zero clue.

The first time I saw it, I just sort of took it in. It's hard to know what tattoo protocol is when you aren't a tattoo person yourself. Is it a private thing, or do people ask, "Hmmm . . . interesting. So what inspired you to create that tat . . . tattoo?" So much learning, always. For example, do you say "tat" or "tattoo"?

My initial instinct was to stay in my comfort zone of uncool but curious and jump right in: "Wow! Is there a story behind what you chose to permanently imprint there on that beautiful, pristine skin of yours, my sweet baby girl?" While that is what I wanted to ask, the actual question that came out of my mouth truncated most of that. Less is more: "Is there a story behind choosing that particular tattoo?"

"Yes, there is, sort of," she replied.

"Hmmm . . . intriguing," I said. "If you'd like to share, go on. And if you don't, that's OK too."

She continued. "It all started with an interview I read online by Andy Puddicombe, one of the founders of Headspace [which created a popular mindfulness app]. When the interviewer asked him what his favorite quote was, he said something about always remembering death and keeping it next to you or by your side. Here's the link; you can read the full version." She pulled it up, and I took a look:

> Thrive Global Interviewer: "Share a quote that you love and that gives you strength or peace."
>
> AP [Andy Puddicombe]: "Keep death by your side." At first this may not sound very inspiring, but one of my Tibetan teachers shared it with me one time and it has stayed with me ever since. The context is that we miss so much of our life because we think that life will go on forever. Because of this, we do not notice each passing moment, we perhaps take others for granted, and we do not appreciate the value of this precious human life.[6]

I have to say, reading this gave me chills. As my *Book of iiwii* pursuit may have suggested by now, I am all about discovering different approaches to life and, in this case, death. I was fascinated.

She went on to say that the skull represents death in the Southwest,

where we live, as well as in many traditions, and that is why she specifically chose it. She also said that there was one other source she read that was a major influence on her decision to choose this particular design and philosophy. It was an article about Nikki Mirghafori, whom I also did not know. After reading about her, I was incredibly impressed. This renaissance woman is: (1) a computer scientist; (2) an artificial intelligence specialist; and (3) a Buddhist teacher.

Hannah told me she especially advocates something called *maranasati*, which basically means, again, always being aware of death. In her article "The Surprising Benefits of Contemplating Your Death"—admittedly not everyone's bedside reading material, but I found myself enthralled—Mirghafori explains:

> Death is something we really don't like to think or talk about, especially in the West. Yet our fear of mortality is what's driving so much of our anxiety, especially during this pandemic. Maybe it's the prospect of your own mortality that scares you. Or maybe you're like me, and thinking about the mortality of the people you love is really what's hard to wrestle with.

> Either way, I think now is actually a great time to face that fear, to get on intimate terms with it, so that we can learn how to reduce the suffering it brings into our lives.[7]

She then goes on to describe some daily reflections that go along with the maranasati approach. There were five reflections, but the one that Hannah said resonated for her was: "Just like everyone, all that is mine, beloved and pleasing, will change, will become otherwise, will become separated from me."[8]

I realized, when I read all this and had my conversation with Hannah, that she had done a mind-blowing job of answering the phenomenal question she had asked herself years earlier: "Enough is enough. What do I need to do not to be that scared girl anymore?" **iiwii?** encourages us not only to ask the hard questions but to do something to both seek and find our own answers.

Sometimes we do have to accept that we just no longer can accept something the way it is. We must do a 180-degree swivel, shift our focus completely around, and unlearn what has always been our go-to strategy. It's reframing our focus. A famous old but still relevant quote from a century ago captures this: "Where your mind goes, energy flows. Whatever you concentrate on you empower." Its author, Ernest Holmes, started an entire movement around the untapped power of our thoughts and beliefs in his revolutionary book *The Science of Mind,* published in the early 1900s.

This theory has been greatly expanded on over the years, with newer voices chiming in, like Bruce H. Lipton's contemporary take in his book *The Biology of Belief,* which says much the same, only now with the benefit of more science to support it. The philosophy supporting **iiwii?** focuses on awareness and creating a vision, supported by belief, that propels us into taking specific steps and tangible measures to create change.

We can choose our own destinations and chart our own unique routes to get there. We don't throw in the towel and use phrases like, ironically, *it is what it is* as an excuse not to take action. When we are in **iiwii?** mode, the belief in our ability to rise above obstacles—including our possible genetic predispositions—and build our vision into reality is paramount. As Lipton asserts, "We are not victims of our genes, but masters of our fates, able to create lives overflowing with peace, happiness, and love."[9]

Hannah had asked the tough question and challenged herself to do the heavy lifting. This, frequently, is frustratingly required when creating strategies to support new ways of being. As she discovered, it wasn't easy, but it wasn't impossible. It could take the form of finally reciting a whole poem successfully in front of her classmates, or it could be the designing of a tattoo as an ever-present reminder of the joy of being a living human (versus being a dead cow skull). For others, it could be something less permanent and profound, like sticking an inspirational quote on our bathroom mirror or deciding to write stories about cousins, storms, and caves. Remember, energy flows where our mind goes.

INSIGHT #1: QUESTION (ASK)

8

∞

Insight #2: Do Something

There may be more to learn from climbing the same mountain
a hundred times than by climbing a hundred different mountains.

—Richard Nelson
(American cultural anthropologist, naturalist, and writer, 1941–2019)

Kicking the Habit

I was a child-teen of the 1970s, a cross of a serious wannabe hippie, a farmgirl hobo, a renegade bareback rider of horses and ponies, a rogue cheerleader, and a junior high hood—in those days, short for *hoodlum*. It was the era of electric-colored eyeshadow, large hoop earrings, and, for me, my Young Life cross necklace. I wore overalls, braids, and bandanas, often paired with my bright orange *Flower Power* short-sleeved sweatshirt.

My bedroom was my haven, a signature part of my expanding identity. Over the years, it came to contain many different things, some sanctioned and some not. It housed a small menagerie of animals, some real but mostly stuffed; collections of various things like troll dolls, glass figurines, and fancy dolls from foreign lands that I dreamed of visiting one day; and my music—a prized stack of 45s, an early and labor-intensive way of listening to music back then on Maggie, my beloved Magnavox record player. This was my sanctuary and was the envy of all who entered, or so I always told myself. Bright yellow and orange flowers splashed across some of the walls, with orange, yellow, and green stripes on the others. There

was a lime-green shag carpet. It was the epic era of the black light and inflatable lounge chairs; I had both.

VICEROYS

I also had other things in my room—things, as I mentioned, that were not sanctioned: my contraband. I am not proud to say this, but I had my first cigarette when I was eleven years old from a stolen pack of Viceroys stashed inconspicuously underneath the red velvet dress of one of the dolls on my shelf. After that first covert cigarette, I never looked back—until the day I did, seven years later. And that cold-turkey day was the response to a question that I could not shake: Why am I smoking these nasty things?

But I am jumping ahead of myself. First, the back story.

My mom was the unknowing Viceroy "dealer" in our household. She was an avid smoker of the brand. I'd like to say she started smoking due to stressful remorse from abandoning her daughter in a forest one day, but that was not the case. Like me, she also had started smoking when she was young.

"I was around twelve or so, up at the farm," she had once let slip to me. In her defense, this was the era of some outrageous advertising around cigarettes. Viceroys, especially, were being lauded as almost healthy, the brand "your dentist would recommend" due to its special new filter system for smoke.[1]

On more than one occasion, she had called cigarettes her "best friend." This is not to make her sound pathetic; she did have lots of other friends who were not cigarettes. That said, it didn't take a brain surgeon, perhaps even one like my father, to realize that this was not a great trait to replicate. And all this was before we even had any idea how bad cigarette smoking was, much less the issue of secondhand smoke.

Recently, I unearthed a long-forgotten and long-hidden photo of my twelve-year-old smoking self. Maybe this is what prompted me to want to write about this. There I was with my long, dark braids, sitting next to some railroad tracks, taking a long drag on my mom's Viceroy. Or maybe, by then, I'd upped my game to Marlboros. We all loved the Marlboro man, or maybe, for me, it was his horse too. I loved them both—and the song.[2] I guess I go for the whole package when I fall in love.

As junior-high years turned into high school, my mom still did not know I had a covert smoking operation up in my (still) bright orange, yellow, and green bedroom. Actually, my sister had joined the fray as well by then. Though I was three years younger, I often felt, even back then, that I was not a good influence on her. Luring her into my bedroom for our first "sisters' cig" is not something I'm proud of. Admittedly, our "habit" was not robust, maybe one or—max—two cigarettes a day, if that. Regardless, it created an opportunity for sibling bonding, or maybe we were just seeing what we could secretly get away with; either way, we had fun!

Gradually, however, over time, our mom did start to wise up to what was going on. She began making this one peculiar comment all the time. It went something like this, while she had a cigarette in her hand, "Oh, I shouldn't be smoking these things. Honey, you should do as I say and not as I do." I would try to knowingly nod, then turn around and wonder if I'd been caught. Then she wouldn't say anything else, so on my merry Marlboro way I'd go.

I've given this phrase quite a bit of thought over the years, especially after I raised kids of my own: "Do as I say, not as I do." You don't hear it as much now, thankfully. It is what we wish would happen without having to go through all or any of the trouble of trying to do it ourselves, much less model it for others. That said, as we all know, it is no small feat to try to quit an addictive behavior. Regarding smoking, new research out of the University of Toronto suggests, "it's more likely it'll take a smoker 30 attempts or more to go a full year without any cigarettes."[3]

There may be more to learn from climbing the same mountain a hundred times than by climbing a hundred different mountains.
—Richard Nelson
(American cultural anthropologist, naturalist, and writer, 1941–2019)

In the same article about quitting smoking quoted above, the writer ponders whether it is helpful or demotivating to know this new statistic on what it takes to kick the smoking habit. Is it helpful to know that you may need to scale that same mountain up to thirty times? Does this motivate

us to want to *do something* and start that first of many hikes up Quitters Mountain or not?

One thing I believe we all do know is that "do as I *do*, not as I say" is where impact resides. Whether we like it or not, we are always a role model to someone. It is *what* we do, not our words, that speaks volumes. A great phrase I heard years ago really nails this: "Your actions speak so loud I cannot hear what you are saying."

Doing something toward taking the first steps to either quitting a bad habit or keeping ourselves from starting one always begins from one place: our thoughts and beliefs about what it is we are trying to do. I honestly believe my mother did not think it was possible for her to stop smoking. "Once a smoker, always a smoker," I vaguely recall hearing her say. I am reminded of a bumper sticker I once saw that simply and appropriately said, "Don't believe everything you think." It's surprising how often we can dupe ourselves by simply believing what we think without even thinking to question it. Who would know anyway?

Counterintuitively, as more and more evidence finally started to emerge as to the dangers of smoking, instead of it becoming easier to quit, I think for many it just became harder. This was compounded by healthy doses of guilt heaped right on top of the self-esteem ash pile, which didn't help either. Sadly, my mom paid the price. Lung cancer stalked her down and, at the way too young age of seventy-one, had its way. In this case, her belief that she couldn't stop played out to be true.

This is why I had to tell the story about Viceroys. It was not something I had remotely intended to include, and yet, for me, the story illustrates how hard it is to challenge our thinking around something we think we cannot change. As I found out, this was exactly when, instead of resigning myself to **iiwii.**, I essentially flipped it to an **iiwii?** and decided to take action before it was too late.

ETCH-A-SKETCH EFFECT

So, as I noted, I developed a plan. My plan was predicated on a thought I had (that did merit belief, in this case) that the easiest time to stop smoking, if I ever was going to do it successfully, was when my world as I knew

it would be undergoing a seismic change. Turning eighteen and leaving home after high school was going to be my springboard.

I have always loved what I thought was one of the great unsung-hero devices of my generation—the Etch A Sketch.[4] I can remember thinking that leaving my world at home would be just like one big shake of an Etch A Sketch: now you see it, now you don't. The screen is blank again, ready for a whole new vista to be carefully etched onto it with a few small little turns of the dials. For me, this idea was exhilarating.

Little did I know that, flash forward forty(ish) years, and this idea would become famous by another name—the fresh-start effect. In her wonderful book *How to Change: The Science of Getting from Where You Are to Where You Want to Be*, author Katy Milkman totally supported my approach. She confirmed that at the point of a major life change, the likelihood of changing a habit has its greatest chance for working and when our efforts to *do something* have the greatest chance of succeeding. She explains:

> The more I've thought about this research, the clearer it's become to me that the potential to harness fresh starts is underutilized. When we hope to change, we have an opportunity to try reshaping our environment to help us disrupt old routines and ways of thinking. This could be as simple as finding a new coffee shop to work in or a new gym. And we should be looking for opportunities to capitalize on other life changes, too, to reevaluate what matters most to us. Whether it's an illness, a promotion, or a move to another town, it could offer just the disruption needed to turn your life around.[5]

She goes on to clarify,

> "Why? Because in these fresh-start moments, people feel more distant from their past failures. Those failures are the old you, and this is the new you. The fresh-start effect hinges on the idea that we don't feel as perfect about our past as we'd like. We're always striving to be better. And when we can wipe out all those failures

and look at a clean slate, it makes us feel more capable and drives us forward.[6]

Invoking what I will now boldly claim and name as the Etch-A-Sketch effect, I took advantage of my, at that point, biggest personal fresh-start moment when I left my home, my city, and my friends and headed off to my new life as a college freshman. I fully knew this was a time when most people would be starting to smoke, not trying to quit. I find, at times, I'm drawn to doing things in upside-down, unconventional ways, so this approach, even back then, had great appeal. And, most importantly, *it worked*. I did it. I stopped.

What was empowering was realizing I could and did make a change. That's not to say that I didn't stack up an impressive list of other vices during my college years (and beyond), but cigarette smoking was not one of them.

In **iiwii.**, we learned from positivity expert Barbara Fredrickson and her team that serenity is what we experience when we allow ourselves the luxury to do nothing, while, interestingly, they discovered it is the emotion or feeling of joy that is linked to the urge to do something—to take action in some direction. She shares with us, "Joy feels light and bright. Colors seem more vivid. There's a spring in your step . . . you feel playful—you want to jump in and get involved. . . . Joy is associated with the urge to do something . . . the active, vibrant and positive embracing or being embraced by circumstances, people in your life."[7]

To refresh, in **it is what it is.**, we are exploring concepts in the context of new learnings. We are learning that *doing nothing* can be a key element of not just surviving but even thriving. In **is it what it is?**, we are unlearning what we have often known or thought we knew to be true. In this case, the theme of *do something* gives rise to the question: Might there be a new course that needs to be charted?

This can be uncomfortable terrain. In thinking about new destinations for ourselves or for some element of our life's journey, it helps to remember nothing needs to happen all at once, and very few things are irreversible. To get started, clear the mental debris first. Then, instead of "carrying in your mind the insane burden of a hundred things that you

will or may have to do in the future," Eckhart Tolle suggests "focusing on the one thing that you can do now."[8]

> **The best time to plant a tree is twenty years ago.**
> **The second-best time is today.**
> —Chinese proverb
> (as quoted in Daniel H. Pink, *The Power of Regret*)

So, even though the status quo may be called "easy" by some (sticking to the same routines, rhythms, and ruts), there are parts that can be very hard, monstrously so at times. This is especially true when we know we should be doing something differently and just cannot seem to figure out where and what our next step should be. "Just focus on the one thing you can do now." I find it helps to recognize and acknowledge an important aha: the world today is rigged for distraction. Why not call it on its bluff?

Just start . . . somewhere. Doing something inspires action.

How I Met Frida

There are two types of doing as I am defining it in this **iiwii?** chapter. One type would be the byproduct of questioning and of choice—questioning what's always been and choosing what might be better. It is made consciously, like questioning our belief that we cannot change something ("We've always been smokers") and then activating the Etch-A-Sketch effect. We actively invoke a clean slate, then pick a point and start turning the dials.

While this type of focused, intentional action or choice is one on-ramp to the *do something* theme of this chapter, the other one is subtler. It is what I call a *choiceless choice*—something needing to be done that just sort of picks us, without our even being conscious of it at the time. We find ourselves drawn, as if by some unseen energetic pull, to do something that comes to us as a complete surprise.

CALL OF THE WILD

This is what happened to me when I first encountered Frida.

Frida is a tree—a mesquite tree, to be exact. I had never heard of

mesquite trees before moving to the desert Southwest twenty years ago. And I felt absolutely no pull at all to understand more about them or any other types of the gnarly, prickly, thorn-laden flora and fauna that inhabited our two-acre yard. Don't get me wrong; I absolutely love the weird, fantastical, Seuss-like cacti of the Sonoran Desert, where we live, even if that sounds mildly contradictory to what I just stated. I just like them from a distance—a very healthy distance.

Like many, before moving here, I had only seen pictures of the tall-with-arms cacti that were always pictured silhouetted against a sunset. Not originally being from these parts, I kind of wondered if they were real or just staged somehow: props photoshopped into southwestern calendars. No, they're real, and so are the outrageously vivid sunsets.

These tallest cacti are called sahuaros or saguaros. People, including me, often wonder about the difference in spelling. Again, back to the Google gods. The difference is that *sahuaro* is an alternative spelling of "saguaro," while *saguaro* is actually the name of the species: *Carnegiea gigantea*, a large cactus native to the Sonoran Desert and characterized by its "arms."

I unabashedly admit that I adore saguaros and have become mildly obsessed with their beauty, history, and quirkiness. I'm even a big fan of prickly pear cacti, especially the purple-hued ones. I'm also nuts for the hugely varied, beautiful, and small succulents (mostly thornless). Jumping chollas, not so much. Yes, they really "jump" at you if you get too close, and they have these barbed balls of thorny spines that latch into you and practically require surgery to dislodge.

I love all these—at a distance, far away from their thorns, spines, needles, hooks, and scratchy parts, whatever the particular name or correct terminology might be. And yet I am a realist. I live in the desert, where these things exist. So in deference to the best-defense-is-a-good-offense line of practical reasoning, I decided to create a desert Thorn Extraction Kit. After lots of testing, the "Kit" finally came to include the following:

- tweezers, an essential thorn-removal tool

- duct tape for quick skin dabbing to get out the tiny, invisible spines
- a large comb to pull a cholla ball off you without touching it
- Prid, a blackish ointment or drawing salve that actually pulls the thorns or splinters out magically(ish)
- a handheld magnifying glass
- a small travel-sized bottle of homeopathic whiskey—dual purpose: to cleanse and sterilize and to swig and numb

For nondesert dwellers, it probably seems silly that I have written out this list. And yet for those of us who do live here, lists like these are actually a godsend. It took me more time than I care to admit, with lots of trial and error, to get all these items identified, tested, and pulled together. If it helps even one other desert dweller somewhere, it will have been worth the time to share it.

So, back to Frida. One of the reasons I especially had zero interest specifically in mesquite trees definitely involved the thorn factor. It turns out that not all of them are thorny, but I didn't know that. For example, doing a quick Google search, this literally is the very first thing that comes up: "Mesquite trees are characterized by their stiff, sharp, pointed thorns. The spikes on thorny mesquite trees grow up to 3" (7.5 cm) long. The strong, stout mesquite spines can cause a lot of pain if you come into contact with them. Mesquite thorns can cause allergic reactions in some people."[9]

Really, need I say more? Actually, I will. In looking at a few more sites, the words "scrubby," "devil tree," "tough," and "ugly" caught my eye. Here is one especially vicious slam: "Early day ranchers like W. T. Waggoner called mesquite 'the devil with roots' because it absorbs all the water in its surroundings, causing other plants and trees to wither away and die. This, in turn, allows more mesquites to move in and take over. Last but not least, this tree has positively vicious thorns."[10]

Why is it that the things we absolutely think we cannot do are the very ones that seem to call out to us? Here's how it all started.

During the standstill of COVID-19, when I was off shift from my

senior-community job, I would come home and decompress by taking walks around our property. With each day, to my great surprise, I started to become more and more mesmerized by the gnarled, untamed, crazy collection of desert plants, trees, and animals that seemed to be everywhere I looked. Even the rocks started calling out to me. I had no idea how many interesting rocks we had: ones streaked with blue copper, striped with red, in unusual shapes and sizes, and on and on.

Can I just state, once again, that I am not the kind of person who ever—well, rarely—notices this kind of nature detail? I'm a nature appreciator, not a nature interactor. I am not a gardener. I do not have a green thumb, though I am trying. I always hated the feel of dirt on my hands; only gloves would do if I had to pot some plants. You get the picture. I had zero desire or interest in any of this calling out to me. And yet other plans were apparently hatching.

The one part of our yard that I *truly* did not have any desire to interact with—as this new interactive pull with nature and my yard was happening—was what I called Jungle West. It gave off the vibe of a modern-day, residential Jurassic Park. Other than a barely recognizable, once rock-lined little trail that Grandpa had made years earlier, there was nothing appealing over there whatsoever. The trail was sort of a nostalgic part of what we now call our ancestral home. Grandpa and Grandma, my husband's parents, had lived in this same desert dwelling home for many years before us. Like me, Grandpa was drawn in his later years to make the transition from nature appreciator to nature interactor. He would have loved the Thorn Extraction Kit.

We all had adored Grandpa, calling him Papa Bear (maybe an unconscious desensitization strategy for my bear-trauma issue?). And yet, the Papa Bear path led to a small, metal storage structure that I would visit only when absolutely necessary. Why? Because along this trail there were millions of dead, jagged branches reaching their black wooden tentacles out everywhere, thorns abounding. Jungle West was a no-man's or woman's land. If you ever saw the movie *The Princess Bride*, there is a scene with a horrifying, super-sized rat-like creature hanging out under some

grizzly looking trees in a forest. If you didn't see the movie, you still get the visual. All I could imagine while trying to stay on the mottled path to get to the shed then quickly pivot and leave, was the possibility that one of these creatures would come running out from this small forest of trees, bushes, twisted staghorn cacti, and jumping chollas and lunge at me.

The worst of it was that, barely visible under one part of the little gnarly forest area, there were not one but two massive packrat nests—mounds of shards of broken nature bits, pieces of trash, and who knows what else—that were the telltale signs of this common desert creature. And these two nests, especially the larger one, easily could have housed a couple of those *Princess Bride* creatures.

So, instead of dinosaurs, our Jurassic Park housed huge rats, definitely rattlers (rattlesnakes) who like to eat the rats, and probably families of javelinas. These boar-sized, prehistoric-looking members of the peccary family have an awful stench and razor-sharp teeth. They are very protective of their own. They have lots of babies and travel in packs. I had, on more than one occasion, seen or smelled some herds of javelinas traversing this west-side area as well. And the potential for rattlesnakes hanging out near the packrats' nests? That speaks for itself.

I realize this is quite the buildup, but it's important to get a clear picture. It makes what happened all the more surprising and nonsensical. One morning, just after Thanksgiving, after months of COVID-19-induced food and drink excess, I felt I had reached an all-time consumption-capacity high. My brain was doing the foggy turkey-brain thing, no doubt, because for some reason I decided to walk over to the west side of the house. I wasn't even needing anything from the shed.

Actually, the thought that had come to me was that maybe, as part of my new getting-to-know-my-yard-and-nature-a-bit-better initiative, I would pick up where Grandpa had left off on his path-building efforts around the property. I would spruce up what he'd done, add new rocks where necessary, realign existing rocks, and blaze some new trails or pathways around the property.

I had the whole visual in my mind. The new paths would wind around

different areas, steering very clear of any thorns angling down or out from their sentient beings: cactus or tree selves. I chose those words carefully, or, just now, they chose me. I had been reading quite a bit about sentient beings and, for some reason, had never really thought of plants and trees as *living beings*. Clearly, they needed air, sun, and water. Even I knew that much. But beyond that? Maybe it was because I was so good at killing them when they were in my care and custody that it was not pleasant for me to think of them, for example, like a dog or small child that I *had* to really try to keep alive. My plants, flowers, and bushes were inanimate, or so I thought. That line of thinking made it perfectly OK when, on many occasions, I had let these things die due to inattention. We don't need one more thing to feel guilty about now, do we?

Well, maybe we do, or maybe I did. On that post-Thanksgiving Day morning, I decided to start my path-reconstruction project. With clear intention, I decided that the place to start was none other than the west side of the house, so I summoned up courage and stamina and marched right over and did an assessment of the pathway. I noticed right away the pattern of rocks, so carefully placed in what were, at one time, perfectly paralleling curves, straightaways, and turns. I could tell it had once been a beautiful, pristine little rock-lined walkway encircling the house.

As I was doing my inspection, seeing if there were more rocks I could find to fill in where needed, I found myself unwittingly going into the forbidding Jungle West precinct. I didn't even realize it until my sweater got snagged on a large creosote bush, one of several that had mysteriously seemed to come forward and encircle me.

I then remembered that my soon-to-be son-in-law Frank, the plant scientist (we didn't have lots to talk about in the early days), was collecting branches of the creosote bush with the small flowering puff balls on them so that he and his students could make and sell small containers of creosote salve. I started breaking off some branches—very gingerly, mind you—and feeling certain that some kind of oily stuff was rubbing off on me and making my hands itch. *I so, so do not like doing this stuff* is something I vividly remember myself thinking as I was doing this. But I loved the kids

and the idea of the project, and I adored his enthusiasm, so I thought, *Suck it up and just do it.* And so I did.

As I was getting a nice little pile of creosote branches ready to take with me back to the path, something caught my eye. In addition to the bushes that seemed to be closing in on me, it appeared that tons of dead branches were almost literally waving at me from what looked like several mesquite trees that were growing up from weird lattices of branches on the ground. Looking more closely, I realized that what I always thought was a forest of these mesquite and palo verde trees (another desert varietal, sporting all-green branches—the name is Spanish for "green stick"—and no thorns) was actually just one very, *very* large mesquite tree with one (not-that-large) palo verde sort of growing underneath it.

It was the most unusual configuration of a tree or trees I had ever seen. Curiously, this is not an uncommon configuration, as I've learned, and it is something incredibly beautiful. Trees become nannies for each other—caretakers of sorts. *Nurse tree* is the actual descriptor. In her blog *All Things Nature,* Mary McMahon defines nurse trees as large, fast-growing trees that provide shelter to smaller trees and plants as they grow.[11] These trees are a critical part of forest ecology all over the world, from the Amazonian rain forest to the tangled Alpine forests of Europe, and they are also ecologically important in some other regions, like the desert. While taking all this in, I was still vigilant in keeping my eye fixed on the massive packrats' nest to my right, rock in hand, in case something jumped out. And yet my curiosity led me forward.

At first, due to the almost opaque cover of dead branches literally going in thousands of different directions, it was impossible to fully take it in. Suddenly, I was on a mission. Truly, a choiceless choice was being made. Against every fiber of my being that wanted to say, "What the heck are you doing, walking right into the mecca of thorniness and who knows what else?" I just kept taking another step forward. It was as though this one very large and unusual tree was inviting me forward. To say it was talking to me sounds over the top, but let's just go there. I felt like it was talking to me.

Given all the things I've shared so far, it is understandable that at about

this point I seriously thought, *I have completely lost it. COVID-19 has officially kicked me over the edge. I am now talking to some branches, or a tree, or whatever.* The next thing it "said" was, "It is OK to break off some of my branches." Maybe it had seen me in my pursuit of the creosote bounty for Frank and had felt a bit jealous? My line of reasoning had already shifted to a new plane: "The tree is talking to me, and now I am ascribing traits of jealousy to her . . . him . . . it?"

I obliged, wincing with an expectation of thorns, itchy oil, and who knows what else might be on these cascading and dense, scraggly branches. I spied a white rock, just barely visible about four yards ahead of me, situated in a place where I knew I could get a better view.

A better view? Was I really doing this? Literally, as they say, with my left hand not knowing what my right hand was doing and me not having any clue of what either hand was doing, I found myself, almost as though hypnotized, breaking off the dead branches of this tree, one by one by one. I had the thought, *Yikes, what am I doing, and, most importantly, am I going to get lacerated by thorns here or what?*

Almost as soon as I had the thought, another thought immediately bubbled up. OK, I'm just going to say it: it was another communication from the mesquite tree. It went something like this: "Do not worry about a thing. I have no thorns or at least none that will prick or hurt you; this I promise. I also promise that these limbs will literally almost fall into your hands. They just need a little help and will break off effortlessly. There are other, bigger ones that also need to go, and I will need your help to get them off me as well. I have been living like this for decades and need to be freed up from all this excess mess."

The tree was truly singing my tune. I continued to break branches. Little ones, shockingly large ones—and, as had been promised, they all literally just fell to the ground with the most minimal of touch. And, miracle of miracles, there was not one single thorn that I felt. Did I mention I did not have gloves on either? My number-one prerequisite for any nature interaction was to be wearing gloves—preferably my pretty flowered Ace Hardware gardening gloves for non-gardeners. The tree reiterated, as if to slow it down for me, "You will not feel any thorns with me."

As my pile of dead mesquite branches was getting higher and higher and my conversation continuing to get more interesting as I closed in on the white rock, I started wondering about tree gender. Thinking that trees are probably gender-neutral, I still decided to pose the question, "Is there a pronoun that you identify with, or will just 'tree' do?" Instantaneously, I got a clear "she."

It's a she. I loved that. Now, what about a name? I didn't even ask if she had a name as I already knew exactly what her name was or was going to be. She had said she wanted to be freed from the heaviness of all this dead weight, and she was a mesquite tree. I would call her Freeda. Freeda the Mesquita (a Spanglish twist) or maybe Frida, Frida Tall-o (an artistic reference twist). I would need to think about it.

She seemed to approve because suddenly I found myself at the white rock, a massive stack of branches behind me, and I wasn't even sure how any of this had happened.

What I then saw next literally sent chills down my spine. She had apparently been hit by lightning or just split somehow (due to the extra weight of all her excessive branches?) right down the middle. Her branches were absolutely magnificent with some arching right down to the ground. Those then gave birth to other branches that grew straight up from them, hence the illusion of a forest of trees. Some of her branches went straight up so high that I was in complete disbelief that I had never noticed this before. What had once looked gnarly and quasi-terrifying now literally took my breath away. Because of the way everything was situated, it felt like a huge protective canopy with a beautiful interior that no human had probably stepped foot in for decades, maybe longer.

It felt like hallowed ground. It almost seemed like she was shimmering with an inexplicable energy.

Just looking at all her no-longer-needed, stifling dead branches lying there, I felt her lightness and my own lightness come together in a kind of interspecies intertwining. She had asked, and I had listened. No matter what species we are, doesn't it, at the end of the day, just kind of boil down to that? Being still, open, listening.

I knew my work was cut out for me, and this was just the beginning.

Whether I wanted to or not, I was out there almost every day through the months of that winter, breaking branches, snapping dead twigs, raking, pruning, and clearing all this stuff off and away from Frida. (I finally did settle on the spelling/name of Frida due to its simplicity and a passion for the amazing painter whose spirit seems kindred to ours.)

The transformation was gradual in some ways and radical in every way. I decided to do as much of the work myself as I possibly could. For the first couple of months, my husband did not even know I was doing this (as I said, none of us went over to Jungle West unless necessary). One day, Hannah, our youngest, strolled out to find me after a few hours of my being missing in action, and I almost had to have her carry me out due to dehydration. Strangely, in the winter in the desert, you need as much, if not more, water than you do in the summer months.

I was learning as much about taking care of myself in some ways as I was about taking care of Frida. And I was getting stronger and bolder. I had even taken on the bigger of the two massive packrat nests, admittedly with some help, but mostly on my own. (I tested out various rat-nest removal techniques on the slightly smaller one first.) Fortunately, there were no gargantuan rats or even little ones residing in this huge domain anymore. They knew their time to relocate had come at the first scent of me hanging out with Frida.

After a month or so, my two daughters and son were in on the freeing Frida project. I think they thought I had been possessed. I didn't blame them. Back to the notion of choices: one of the things that kept hitting me over and over again was the idea that at no point had I ever really chosen to do this, nor, if asked, would I have ever agreed to do so.

Whether it is a connection to an animal, a human, or a tree, sometimes there is a choiceless choice. No matter what, it has claimed you, and you have claimed it. While some of these connections can be utterly life-sustaining, others can be ill-advised, unconventional, or even downright dangerous. When my husband found out I had covertly bought and been using a chainsaw in our backyard, I will admit he almost flipped a grit. So did our son. They are both a bit protective. My daughters were all

in. Kristen, our oldest, who happened to be stranded in town during the pandemic, became my chainsaw spotter and helped me get the last of the bigger branches pruned and pretty.

I have come to learn that there is a scientific term for what was taking place during this entire Frida encounter. It is called *biophilia* and refers to a deep need humans have to be connected to nature and the release of a strong shot of feel-good molecules that can happen as a result. So maybe I wasn't just imagining this strange pull. I certainly wasn't imagining how good I gradually started to feel every time I was out interacting with Frida and her friends.

Gradually, my grumbling, "There is no way this is going to work," started to dissipate. With each new clearing of branches and stacking of mile-high resulting debris, the utter impossibility of this started to recede as a new sense of possibility inched forward. Without ever knowing it, I was knee deep in **iiwii?** territory.

"Am I really doing this? Is it what it is?" I asked.

"Yes, you are, and yes, it is" was the reply.

Just keep swimming. Or pruning. Ask the questions, then get going, and do it.

People have secrets for how they do this. I learned one of these recently at a celebration of life for a get-it-done guru, a hugely talented and beloved community leader named Margaret. Her family shared her simple secret: "Every morning I wake up and eat the frog."

I will admit, for a moment, it was a head-scratcher. And then it was such a lovely aha. Tackle the unpleasant, slimy, undesirable stuff first, right at the beginning of your day. Then it's done.

In the landmark book *Mindset,* Carol Dweck presents the concept of a growth mindset,[12] in which consistent effort, curiosity, and persistence (and probably frog-eating) are encouraged and celebrated. She stresses that this is always an ideal way to approach life, but it is especially important in the face of difficult tasks, failure, or the threat of failure.

For a moment, let's look at a couple of perspectives from two people who both, in extremely different ways, exemplify a growth-mindset per-

spective. First, from J. K. Rowling: "It is impossible to live without failing at something unless you live so cautiously that you might as well not have lived at all, in which case you have failed by default."[13]

OK, a bit of an ice dump over the head with that one. On to the next, from Nelson Mandela: "Do not judge me by my successes; judge me by how many times I fell down and got back up again."[14]

The opposite of a growth mindset is, not shockingly, a fixed mindset, one I believe Dweck and many would say is trending heavily in much of our Western outlook and culture right now. It is the opposite of the appeal that Rowling and Mandela make to us. It is the one-and-done approach: "I tried; I failed; it must not work—at least for me." "If I don't nail it right away, what's the point?" "Never let them see you sweat." I must admit, the reason it was so easy for me to rattle off all those imaginary retorts so quickly is that, at one time or another, I confess to having employed them all.

iiwii? pushes us toward bravery, nudging us out of inertia, even if we don't feel like it. It asks us to imagine a destination and get started gently. It begins with a subtle internal shift that doesn't happen until there is some movement—even if it is just the pace of snails in captivity. We are moving into a space where perhaps we must reject "the way it is" and instead *do something*. Take even just a small, tiny step in the direction of our vision. Rearrange some rocks on a path. Clear some branches. Make a decision to finally replace that nasty habit with a better one and start drawing our map or designing our GPS route.

When we infuse **iiwii?** with **iiwii.**, great things can happen. **iiwii.** first gives us the tools for a growth-mindset world: curiosity, an open heart, serenity, and acceptance. Then we can more easefully move toward empowered action through **iiwii?**, creating our destination, knowing the route can contain obstacles, and yet being fluid and flexible. At this point, it's not getting caught up in and distracted by all the details, rumination, pluses and minuses, or to-do lists that we can spend hours on. It is having the courage to try without having all the answers or hardly any of them as to how this will work out. The door has opened, and it's waiting for us to walk through it. Opportunity has a shelf life; don't wait too long.

As a lovely postscript to the Frida story, while my daughter and I were

co-conspirators in freeing Frida and she was making sure the only limbs that got chainsawed off belonged to a tree and not her mother, Kristen made an offhanded comment—something about people saying wedding vows under trees. *Hmmm . . . curious*, I thought, but said nothing.

Who would have thought, just seven months later, that Frida would invite us all to a wedding reception? It would be right there in her sacred, inner sanctuary of natural love with her cleared and buoyant branches embracing us all, shimmering with excitement and beauty. That's right: Kristen and Frank, the creosote-salve creator / plant scientist, got married. While the wedding ceremony happened in a small chapel, what they called their *ancestral vows of love and commitment* were said while the newlyweds were literally standing on a large branch at the very spot where Frida had once been broken in two. Out of our greatest wounds often spring our greatest healings and blessings. Fairy lights, friends, family . . . and Frida. *Magical* does not even begin to describe it.

INSIGHT #2: DO SOMETHING (ACTION)

9

∞

Insight #3: Build It

If we worked on the assumption that what is accepted as true
really is true, then there would be little hope for advance.

—Wilbur and Orville Wright
(American inventors, pioneers of modern aviation,
Wilber:1867–1912; Orville: 1871–1948)

Wilbur and Orville:
My Grandmother's Neighbors

On Tuesday, May 30, 1899, Wilbur Wright, sitting at his sister Katharine's desk in Dayton, Ohio, handwrote a request to the Smithsonian Institution. This short communication has been called one of the most important letters ever written in history. Wilbur wrote and shared that "ever since a boy,"

> I have been interested in the problem of mechanical and human flight. . . . My observations since have only convinced me more firmly that human flight is possible and practicable . . .

> I am about to begin a systematic study of the subject in preparation for practical work to which I expect to devote what time I can spare from my regular business. I wish to obtain such papers as the Smithsonian Institution has published on this subject, and if possible, a list of other works in print in the English language.[1]

This letter, addressed to Richard Rathburn, then head of the Smithsonian, was the first domino in a very long line of thousands of dominos

that ultimately led to arguably one of the greatest inventions of all times: a way to make it possible for humans to fly.

Have you given thought recently to how much we quite simply take for granted when we hear about space travel or look up into the sky and see a jet flying overhead, bound for destinations mysterious and unknown—and possibly exotic? In the timeline of humankind's existence, it is just a short blip ago that the thought of people in flight, much less as passengers of something called an "airplane" that could safely and reliably transport anyone or anything, was preposterous.

CRAZY BOYS

Up until the point when Wilbur decided to write his letter, many attempts had been made to build what were, at the time, simply called "flying machines." The general consensus, literally around the world, was that humans were just not meant to fly. This had become known and decided, *among those who knew*, to be a "universal truth":

> Along with the cost of experiments in flight, the risks of humiliating failure, injury, and, of course, death, there was the inevitable prospect of being mocked as a crank, a crackpot, and in many cases with good reason.

> For more than fifty years, or long before the Wright brothers took up their part, would-be "conquerors of the air" and their strange or childish flying machines, as described in the press, had served as a continuous source of popular comic relief.[2]

Not only was flying deemed an impossibility, but it also was becoming the target of great ridicule. Many had tried and failed spectacularly. There had been inventions with the "pilot" strapped into a chair with wings that had umbrellas for ascension. There had been gliders reminiscent of large ducks, huge and unusual kite-type creations, and, most notable for its uniqueness, something called the *aerostat* that looked like a long flying fish with front and back V-shaped wings that resembled large dragonflies.[3]

Meanwhile, back in Dayton, Ohio, in June 1895, my grandmother Marjorie was born, apparently not too far away from 7 Hawthorne Street,

where, in her words, "two crazy boys lived that kept building these con-traptions and flying and crashing them in fields on the edge of town." So I have first-hand information that, yes, in fact, even little seven-year-old girls down the street, one of whom I am related to, thought these two were nut cases.

And yet maybe it's because my grandmother knew them (sort of) and then, by the associative power of relatedness, I, in a small way, (sort of) know them too, that the more I've gotten to know about them, the more I have become obsessed with their story and with two questions in particular: Why these two, and how did they do it?

Wilbur and Orville, who they were and what they accomplished, rep-resent and capture the heart of the **iiwii?** philosophy. They started with the question **is this really what is?**, or might there be more? Although many others had already tried and failed in attempts to take flight, might there be another way? As cited earlier, the brothers had made this telling statement early on: "If we worked on the assumption that what is accepted as true really is true, then there would be little hope for advance."[4]

Essentially, they asked and answered the question "When is enough enough?" Their response was a resounding "It is time to go for it. Crazy or not, here we come." They had the insight to question what was then considered "truth," accepting that they *no longer could accept* that humans in flight was impossible. They had the courage to do something about it—a very *empowered* something. This level of doing would require a whole new level of effort, collaboration, courage, and persistence to get flight across the finish line.

And it would require something else, ever so briefly mentioned in Wilbur's letter to the Smithsonian. In his phrase "a systematic study of the subject," Wilbur provided a clue, whether he knew it or not, that later became the stealth ingredient in why I believe they were finally so success-ful—the answer to my question #2: *How* did they do it? Stay tuned, and we will discover what that is after we learn the answer to my question #1: Why these two?

The more I read about these two men, the more it became apparent

that if there were ever two people who had what it took to pull off something like this, it was Wilbur and Orville Wright. Octave Chanute, a renowned aeronautics, physics, and engineering Yoda of the day, told the brothers it was as if they were "pursued by a blind fate"[5] from which they were unable to escape. Choiceless choice reappears.

A great statesman from my esteemed home state of Missouri, William Danforth, spoke eloquently about navigating such situations that seem to have a relentless, magnetic pull. His wisdom was to "say yes." To underscore this, he challenges us by saying, "I dare you while there is still time to have a magnificent obsession."[6] For me, it had been liberating a tree and writing this book. For the Wright brothers, it was the birth of the entire industry of aviation. Sort of a parallel there, no?

So, in answering the question "why these two?" not surprisingly, much has been written on the topic. I will attempt to summarize some of the brothers' standout traits, especially those that highlight key **iiwii?** attributes.

Apparently, Wilbur and Orville both had a tremendous sense of humor and an insatiable appetite for learning, loved figuring out how things worked, were relentless and resilient, and, most significantly, were inseparable their whole lives. They were a formidable team.

For the brothers, community was everything. Both were extremely close to their family, especially their parents and younger sister, Katharine. These younger three Wright siblings (there were five in total, with older brothers Lorin and Reuchlin having married and moved away) were known to their friends as Will, Orv, and Katie.[7] Katharine was often referred to as the "third Wright Brother."[8] She would prove invaluable to them later in terms of emotional, administrative, and home-front support.

In addition to their very close-knit family, the manner in which they were able to grow up contributed to their success in a huge way, especially when we consider the concept of the growth mindset discussed previously in the Frida story. In later years, when queried about their successes, Orville said, "We were lucky enough to grow up in an environment where there was always enough encouragement for children to pursue intellectual interests; to investigate whatever aroused curiosity. In a different kind

of environment, our curiosity might have been nipped long before it could have borne fruit."[9]

From the time he was a young boy, Wilbur had especially been mesmerized by the idea of becoming airborne—how things navigated going up and down in the air. He would literally spend hour upon hour just watching birds fly. He was especially entranced with albatrosses.[10]

His younger brother, Orville, was a genius mechanically, very business minded, and, along with Wilbur, had a photographic memory. He also was, of the two, the more cheerful and optimistic, yet he experienced "peculiar spells" when he could get very moody, brooding, irritable, and overwhelmed for a bit, then rebound.[11] For Orville, navigating these bouts of what today we probably would call anxiety or an anxiety-/stress-related disorder was not easy; they were setbacks he had to learn to overcome.

In a similar—and similarly not well-known—vein, Wilbur had his own demons to deal with. While his father had said early on that the elder brother was "never rattled," there was a severe accident that left him extremely rattled and dramatically changed the course of his life.

Historian David McCullough shares in his iconic book *The Wright Brothers* that in, or around 1887, a neighborhood bully and deranged kid, Oliver Crook Haugh, profoundly changed the path of Wilbur's life when he intentionally smashed Wilbur in the face with a hockey stick. It happened one unfortunate winter afternoon during a pickup game of ice hockey on a pond in their neighborhood. Oliver's stick caused major damage. Wilbur was supposed to finish high school later that year, but the resulting brain injury left him not only without the achievement of graduating from high school, but it also dashed his hopes of studying at Yale University, which there had been much talk of him attending.[12]

For a few years after the incident, Wilbur rarely left his home. He was trying to navigate huge bouts of depression triggered by the injury while also becoming the primary caregiver to his very beloved mother, who had become terminally ill.

The reason I highlight these seemingly random points about anxiety and setbacks is that these are often some of the number-one indicators I

have found when doing an **iiwii?**, that we are counterintuitively on the right track. Both in the beginning of a new initiative and especially at the end, everything under the sun that can drop obstacles in our path seems to be called forth. Instead of giving in or giving up, the **iiwii?** objective is to find ways either to dodge the obstacles or, if that is impossible, to make such setbacks work for, as opposed to against, us.

So while both brothers had what was often touted to be "unity of purpose and unyielding determination"[13] as part of their own magnificent obsession with flight, they also had some very tricky personal obstacles to overcome before they even really got started. This is the behind-the-scenes stuff that people never or rarely talk about. All of us experience setbacks. No one gets a free pass. And yet these, at times, can ironically be just the fuel we need to get the process started.

ANXIETY ANTIDOTE

In the chapter entitled "Do Nothing" in **iiwii.**, I referenced the intriguing idea that sometimes the "problem can be the solution."[14] It was through this filter that I was drawn to an article in 2022 in the New Books section of the Sunday paper. The essay, entitled "In Praise of Anxiety: Using Anxiety to Survive and Thrive,"[15] was written by Tracy Dennis-Tiwary, author of a newly published book, *Future Tense: Why Anxiety Is Good for You (Even Though It Feels Bad).*[16] In this essay, which gives readers a sneak peek into her book on the benefits of anxiety, she states, "We need to create a new mindset about this misunderstood emotion. Reframing and reclaiming anxiety as an advantage and a valued part of being human isn't easy or just a matter of willpower. It takes practice and time, and it doesn't mean that anxiety becomes enjoyable. Anxiety can't do its job unless it makes us uncomfortable, forcing us to sit up and pay attention. We don't need to like anxiety—just to use it in the right way."[17]

She is very careful to make a distinction between anxiety and anxiety disorder—the latter being diagnosed by a physician, she disclaims, needing separate protocols and treatment. She goes on to explain that anxiety can actually give us a dopamine hit, releasing the feel-good chemical in our

brain that we usually associate with something fabulous happening, like winning the lottery, falling in love, or getting a text from a favorite friend.

Apparently, research has found that dopamine is also released when we step up to a challenge, when we say yes (even to ourselves) to doing something when every fiber of our being is crying out, "No way!" It would be agreeing to do something that is incredibly uncomfortable, something we'd typically consider highly stressful and far more harrowing than rewarding.

I experienced this "I can't" feeling firsthand when, not once but twice, I was asked to speak at the funerals of two of my all-time favorite people, each of whom died way too soon. They are mentioned in the beginning of this book, two of my "four formidables," JoAnne and Georganne. These brief stories merit a quick detour.

At the time of the first request, my fear meter about speaking in front of others was probably a fifteen out of ten. Added to this was the complexity, pressure, and yet profound honor that JoAnne had specifically asked me, her "favorite troublemaker," during our last conversation together to stand up and "say a little something" at what I knew would be a large funeral service congregation. JoAnne, in addition to Anne, my mother, raised me literally from birth. She took me out on my twenty-first birthday to buy me my "first cocktail" at Milton's jazz club and joined me for my bachelorette party a few years later. She was a Black woman who broke every mold there was, and I could not have loved her more.

The dreaded day arrived, and the church was absolutely packed. There were a handful of white faces in the crowd, but the rest were Black, beautiful, and as sad as I was to lose this amazing member of the human race. I took my place up front at the allotted time, and somehow I made it through what I wanted to say. I kept it light, very short, and heartfelt. After I finished, my only memory was of somehow reaching my spot in the pew and then disintegrating into a grieving heap next to my two brothers, my dad, and Sis. I was a mess, but I had done it.

For Georganne, it was years later. Fortunately, I was not terrified of speaking in public anymore, but I was completely overwhelmed with sadness and pain at her way-too-early death. She was my younger cousin by a year and, like JoAnne, had been a kindred spirit. I completely adored her.

Both Georganne and JoAnne would be great examples of a key element of the **iiwii?** spirit. They were fiercely independent yet realized the importance of connection, whether to a two- or a four-legged community of like-minded souls. I admired them both for this. I started Georganne's eulogy with my earliest memory of something she loved to say: "I'd rather do it myself." I ended JoAnne's with a similar piece of wisdom she had once shared with me: "Love many, trust few, always paddle your own canoe."

So was it dopamine I felt after I made it through both of these intensely anxiety-producing situations? I'm not sure, but it certainly felt like a hit of something. I felt a deep sense of pride and gratitude for having truly dug deep, allowing my love for these two to override all the inner noise that said I couldn't. Life asks us, frustratingly and agonizingly at times, to do what needs to be done and to get over ourselves, our fears, and that voice that says, "I can't." Here is a beautiful **iiwii?** reply to that: "Actually, I can."

It was this antidote of using anxiety versus *letting it use us* that served to help Wilbur and Orville as well. In addition to all the other things they had going for them, it is quite possible that one of their greatest sources of motivation came from what essentially were their greatest obstacles and toughest times. Fighting to overcome anxiety (and later an almost fatal bout of typhoid fever) for Orville and depression from the horrific accident and the ensuing death of his mother (Susan Wright died of tuberculosis in 1889) for Wilbur certainly could have put them both in some very altered, anxious states.

Many say that had Wilbur not experienced this time of dropping out of the flow of life for a while, their trajectory toward becoming the brothers who invented modern flight would not have happened. Wilbur gradually emerged from this stretch of time where he basically needed to just do an **iiwii. it is what it is.** Accepting it first, he allowed himself to move through it on his own terms. He had to *do nothing* for a while. It was truly a period in his life when he needed to step back and just let things be.

He needed to accept that his life was not going to go in the direction he had planned (prestigious East Coast university and whatever that might have brought him), his mother was gone, and he and his brother would

have to make a viable business out of their bike shop to support them-selves. There is a thoughtful comment Wilbur made that seems to apply to this challenging time. It was: "Do not let yourself be forced into doing anything before you are ready."[18]

Gradually, step by step, Wilbur began to get himself untangled. He replenished his energy and caught his wave. Not unlike the process of our **iiwii.** analogy of logs in a logjam, an unobtrusive, imperceptible flow of life and energy seemed to loosen things up for him. Finally, he was ready.

Wilbur Wright began to step back into life, take his place next to his brother, and really dive into making their bicycle business a success for one major reason—so that the bike business could support his true passion, their mutual magnificent obsession and life purpose: starting in earnest to crack the code on how to get humans reliably and safely up in the air. They had asked the question "**is it what it is?**" They were doing something, making their plans, assembling their team, and now they were ready to build it.

> *God grant me the freedom of a well-defined structure.*
>
> —Craig Lueck
> (Hallmark illustrator and American watercolor painter)

PITCH, ROLL, AND YAW: A SYSTEM BORN

So how did they build their vision; how did they do it? In the same way, an artist creates a structure and even boundaries, especially in watercolor, for where the paint will and won't go, so the same approach is needed for any invention or great endeavor. The framework is created so that the color and/or creative experimentation can be applied freely to finish the painting or, in the case of the Wright brothers, help build their system.

Determined to be much more than two-bit hacks, cranks, or amateurs, Wilbur and Orville hunkered down for the next few years, trying to gather information on everything that had been done—what had worked (birds) and what had not worked (all human effort up to that point)—and, in essence, force themselves to unlearn it all and start over. Talk about an Etch-A-Sketch fresh start. They immersed themselves. Obsession had pos-

sessed them, and they and their team submerged themselves in the process of trial and error, testing then failing, retesting and learning, over and over.

Based on everything written about the brothers, it cannot be stressed enough how important were the support and collaboration of each other and their friends and family. They had a very close-knit, equally obsessed crew of motley individuals, both back in Dayton and eventually at their second home (a wooden shed by a sand dune) in Kitty Hawk, North Carolina. Both brothers were known to have said, "What one man can do himself directly is but little. If, however, he can stir up ten others to take up the task, he has accomplished much."[19]

The right people were assembled, and it was the perfect time to take the "systematic study of the subject" (from Wilbur's original letter to the Smithsonian) to a whole new level. In addition to persistence, anxiety-fueled resiliency, and the collaboration of many, this excerpt from that early letter also points to one key and fundamentally crucial **iiwii?** word: *systematic*. This, I believe, is what finally separated Wilbur and Orville and their efforts from all those who had tried and given up before them.

It is in his choice of words that Wilbur gave us an early spoiler alert to the fact that even when he was wanting simply *to study* something (like his magnificent passion of birds and flight), he needed it to be a *systematic* process. Both Wilbur and Orville were early versions of what we would call systems thinkers today.[20]

They asked questions like: "How do all the parts integrate into a model that is sustainable and repeatable?" They were not interested in the one-and-done approach of many of their predecessors. They wanted to understand it all: how every single piece of this flying puzzle fit together so that eventually it wouldn't matter who was flying it, what the machine looked like, or what the weather conditions might be. All that mattered was that, ultimately, *none* of that would matter.

While Orville was the mechanical mastermind, it was Wilbur who was the integrator, the one to realize that a reliable, fully tested, fully comprehensible system was absolutely necessary to make flight possible:

What the Wright brothers accomplished in four years other

would-be aeronauts had been attempting for decades. The brothers distinguished themselves by realizing that what a flying machine needed was a pilot with complete control over the machine, and a machine that would allow itself to be completely controlled. Their wing-warping biplane, the *Flyer*, was the first powered airplane that enabled the pilot to control the craft's pitch, roll, and yaw—its movements along the three axes of rotation: lateral, longitudinal, and vertical.[21]

To simplify, they found their system. The three words—*pitch, roll,* and *yaw*—refer to the three types of movements that occur with anything, like an albatross, that has managed to take flight in the air. Is the beak up or down (pitch)? Are the wings tilted left or right (roll)? When landing on a branch, what is its body's relationship to the horizon? How can it center itself and reorient its wings, especially if the wind is blowing them side to side (yaw) so the landing happens exactly on the preferred branch instead of, for example, smashing into the trunk of a tree? These distinct types of rotational "systems" are what Wilbur discovered during his untold hours of watching birds, both as a youth and as he was recovering from his injuries. Doing his own version of an **iiwii.**, he took time to be still and to see what was actually taking place. No one had ever taken the time to notice these and understand that they were, in simple 1-2-3 fashion, the underlying foundations of flight for a bird and, as it turned out, for anything that wanted to successfully become airborne.

With pitch, roll, and yaw, they had the framework for their system. From there, more order and structure were established as they built their engine from scratch (a lighter-weight version of the new car engines of the day) and tested hundreds of different materials for the wings, propellers, guts, and skin of the machine. It was the essence of experimentation, of trial and error.

At their impressive memorial in Kitty Hawk, somehow all this came together for me with one easily missed knee-level plaque at the base of a very tall grassy hill. The brothers used to drag their different flying machines up this massive hill, which now has a large, majestic monument

on top of it. They used this sand dune as a hilltop takeoff/launch pad for their attempted flights or "glides," which they often called them. The description of the site states, "Climbing the hill was strenuous. Deep, soft sand caused every step up the slope to slip partway back down. The Wrights were also burdened with carrying their heavy gliders up the hill for each flight. Their tireless efforts paid off as they mastered their flying skills and refined their flight controls."[22]

They were into it for the pure joy of doing something they loved, and that made them feel invigorated. They never gave up, and they never ever lacked new ideas on how something might be slightly changed or, alternatively, totally scrapped and replaced with something entirely different.

Once again, the book *Mindset* becomes relevant. Dweck provides an apt description of what was taking place: "Important achievements require a clear focus, all-out effort, and a bottomless trunk full of strategies. Plus, allies in learning."[23]

As mentioned before, she is a huge advocate of cultivating a growth mindset, one that is perfectly captured in basically everything the Wright brothers did and were about. They had their squad, their "allies in learning" *and* in launching *and* in picking up debris of broken planes—a loyal team who would, with humor and grace, embody the beautiful Benedictine phrase "always, we begin again."[24] They had focus and all-out effort in spades. They had perseverance, ingenuity, and a tenacity for trying and failing, over and over again.

In the words of John T. Daniels, one of their Kitty Hawk crew, the Wrights were "'two of the workingest boys' ever seen, 'and when they worked, *they worked* . . . They had their whole heart and soul in what they were doing.'"[25]

They discovered a way of building simulated wind tunnels to test their materials and structures. When there were no automobile engines to be found that were lightweight enough or suited for their needs, they had their beloved guru mechanic back in their Dayton bike shop build them one. They transported materials, engine prototypes, and all sorts of wing, wheel, propeller, and flying parts back and forth by train between Dayton

and Kitty Hawk. From the beginning, they had begun with the end in mind. They were getting very close.

Even though the number of their attempts, failures, and reattempts in getting airborne was growing by the thousands (in one thirty-six-day stretch in the fall of 1902, the brothers estimated they made between seven hundred and one thousand glides, increasing their distance to just over six hundred feet), the Wright brothers' efforts were still largely unnoticed by anyone. They had used a lovely under-the-radar strategy to do all their practical and tactical work in the nearly vacant Outer Banks. This had afforded them the time and privacy to focus, experiment, fail, and succeed outside of the critical judgment of the public eye or much of anyone's eye, for that matter.

That said, while they were cloistered in Kitty Hawk, other efforts toward the coveted first official flight achievement were gaining momentum. One of these efforts specifically stands out and merits mentioning. It was epic—and, sadly, not in a good way. It was called one of the worst personal failures of the twentieth century:

> Samuel P. Langley . . . was a decorated professor of physics and mathematics, and president of the Smithsonian Institute. . . . In 1898, he was given $50,000 dollars by the US War Department, and we *should* know him as the man who invented flight. In 1903, Langley made several very public attempts at flight that failed miserably. And after being utterly humiliated by the *New York Times*, he gave up on his dream in an attempt to save his reputation. Only days later, history was written when the Wright brothers succeeded where the esteemed professor had failed. The difference between Langley and the Wright brothers was this—*a fundamental difference in mindset*. Langley's ego went into self-preservation mode—he was crippled by fear and shame, which prevented him from reaching his true potential. I wonder what else he might have accomplished if he were able to laugh at his critics, learn from this experience, and try again?[26]

John Maxwell, in his book *Failing Forward*, devotes an entire chapter to

Langley's humiliation only days before the famous first flight achieved by my grandmother's "Dayton boys" and their team in Kitty Hawk. Maxwell uses the story to show how the fear of failure, including too much concern with what others think, can become the greatest obstacle of all to success and to getting something over the finish line.[27] This would be the opposite of an **iiwii?** approach.

In Carol Dweck's (*Mindset*) terminology, this would be a textbook example of her notion of a "fixed mindset." While we often easily ascribe it to others and often to *any* generation but our own, we are all prey to its clutches. It is the trumping of ego over exploration, concern with the optics of a situation, not the lessons learned. "I should have figured this out." "It is I, not the experiment, that is the failure." "Collaboration is overrated, and it's easier just to do it myself." Did you catch a wee bit of **iiwii.** self-shoulding there?

Meanwhile, back at the Kitty Hawk sand dunes, the thousands of hours of hard work were finally paying off for our growth-mindset superheroes Orville and Wilbur. They had their system. They had a motor that was light enough, yet strong enough to get them airborne from ground-level terrain (no gliding off the top of the sand dune this time!). They had their crew. The weather cooperated. And one morning in mid-December, it happened:

> It was 12 seconds that would change the world forever. On the cold, windy morning of December 17, 1903, on the sandy dunes of Kitty Hawk, North Carolina, a small handful of men gathered around a homemade mechanical contraption of wood and fabric. They were there to witness the culmination of years of study, trial and error, sweat and sacrifice made by two humble, modest men from Dayton, Ohio. That day, the Wright Brothers' dreams of flight would come to fruition, as Orville Wright took to the sky for 12 bumpy seconds.[28]

"I like to think about that first airplane, the way it sailed off in the air as pretty as any bird you ever laid your eyes on. I don't think I ever saw a prettier sight in my life," eye-witness John T. Daniels later recalled.[29]

As an aside, I found the following fascinating as a sort of footnote to

the whole thing: "Not incidentally, the Langley project had cost nearly $70,000, the better part of it public money, whereas the brothers' total expenses from everything between 1900 and 1903, including materials and travels to and from Kitty Hawk, came to a little less than $1,000, a sum paid entirely from the modest profits of their bicycle business."[30]

After performing a quick click or two of research, I learned that $70,000 in 1903 is equivalent in purchasing power to about $2,400,000 today. Regarding the Wright brothers' personal tab, $1,000 in 1903 would be equivalent to about $34,000 in today's dollars. Fascinating and shocking, all in one.

CHECKLIST MANIFESTOS AND EMERGENT STRATEGIES

One essential characteristic of modern life is that we all depend on systems—on assemblages of people or technologies or both—and among our most profound difficulties is making them work.

—Atul Gawande, *The Checklist Manifesto: How to Get Things Right*
(Indian-born American surgeon, writer, and public-health researcher)

While a general blueprint or outline may work for art, airplanes, or even creating new habits, when chaos reigns, we may need to go one step further. Checklists, at least for me, become imperative. I acknowledge that often they can feel rigid and the opposite of the *go with the flow* we enjoy in **iiwii.** mode. And yet now we are in **iiwii?** territory, which encourages us to become intentional about unlearning the ways that may have once worked but now perhaps need tweaking or demolishing. **iiwii?** challenges us to think about new ways of questioning, doing things, and creating systems, like the Wright brothers did, that are innovative, purposeful, and sustainable.

Boundaries, personal and collective, figure prominently when in **iiwii?** mode. We try not to let egos take over. Sound systems and structures make us feel secure. We know what the parameters are—where we can and can't paint, so to speak. Everyone is assembled in place and has a role. While a system is being created, figuring out the highest and best use

of each participant's time and talent is a critical part of making the system work. Who is doing what, when?

In his book *The Checklist Manifesto: How to Get Things Right*,[31] Atul Gawande does an excellent job emphasizing this fairly obvious yet surprisingly neglected element of creating and minding a process: adhering to system parameters that have (for very important reasons) been established—like, for example, with brain surgery. Get the basics down: simple, clear, and in priority order. He advocates creating simple checklists, timelines, and people assigned to doing the items on the list. In the world of **iiwii.**, timelines are not essential or, often, even necessary. In the world of **iiwii?**, timelines are imperative.

Ironically, back to our aviation focus, Gawande uses the example of flight manuals as a critical prototype. Nothing can be left to chance or interpretation. Down to the absolute basics, it's not *person-dependent* but system-dependent. Unlike **iiwii.**, there is zero room for mystery or uncertainty here. To build and construct a sustainable system that can transport millions of people safely across oceans, we cannot afford to wing it.

Ultimately, the success of a venture cannot ride on the expertise, ingenuity, or personality of any one person and be sustainable over time. It must ride on the integrity of the system as a whole. If something happens to that one central player and there is no backup, the game is over. It has to be simplified to a checklist, a map, or core elements so that basically anyone, with some coaching, can follow what has been mapped out. There is a growing field, recognizing an age-old phenomenon, that builds on this idea, called *emergence*:

> Emergence is what happens when a multitude of little things—neurons, bacteria, people—exhibit properties beyond the ability of any individual, simply through the act of making a few basic choices: Left or right? Attack or ignore? Buy or sell? The ant colony is the classic example, of course. This meta-organism possesses abilities and intelligence far greater than the sum of its parts: The colony knows when food is nearby, or when to take evasive action, or, amazingly, just how many ants need to leave the colony to forage for the day's food or ward off an attack.[32]

In the book *Emergent Strategy*, adrienne maree brown goes one step further and encourages us to remember that "everywhere there is complex, ancient, fertile ground full of potential."[33] So if the spirit moves you, go out and assemble your team. Try, fail, and try again until you get it "Wright" (couldn't resist). Create a framework that works for everyone, and we will all be celebrating, just like my grandmother, Marjorie, did later when she finally praised "those two crazy neighbors" for becoming the brilliant forces behind what she unabashedly felt was "the single most important invention of modern times."

Never doubt that a small group of thoughtful, committed citizens can change the world: indeed, it's the only thing that ever has.

—Margaret Mead
(American cultural anthropologist, author and speaker, 1901–1978)

INSIGHT #3: BUILD IT (ASSEMBLE)

10

∞

Transformation: iiwii?
Ancestral Healing

In the distance a hum, the soft sound of people waking up:
waking up to what is possible for the earth at this sensitive
juncture; waking up to the call that is coming from our
ancestors and from future generations, a call to awaken.

—The Turning Tide Coalition
(as quoted in Lynne Twist, *The Soul of Money*)

The Great Unlearning

Ancestral healing is one of those phrases that can have as many different meanings as there are people to try to explain those meanings. Circling back to my daughter Hannah's earlier question regarding my credentials for explaining such lofty concepts, again I assert that it is precisely because I am unqualified that I feel oddly qualified. Unbound by others' theories, I am free to play around with making up my own.

To start, when I use the word *ancestral,* it is loose. I use it to refer to family members from my own well-charted lineage (thanks to my genealogically obsessed grandmother and mother), my current family members, and my friends whom I consider family due to my close bonds with them (you all know who you are). Also, it includes people like Anne Lamott, Eckhart Tolle, Byron Katie, Albert Einstein, and last but certainly not least Wilbur and Orville Wright, to each of whom I *wish* I were related.

Next, the word *healing* has context for me that might make its usual connotation a bit different. I have learned that, especially in Eastern medical realms, the word *integration* is often used instead of *healing*. The idea is that for someone to become well, a part of our body to become fixed, or a disease to be cured, the process that takes place is an all-encompassing coming together of many different mind/body/spirit puzzle pieces that then bring our whole being into a place of wellness. The pieces have all found their spots, and the whole picture emerges naturally with alignment or healing as the result.

For me, the experience of writing this book has felt like an alignment. The gathering, writing, and sharing of my favorite pieces of wisdom, quotes, theories, and legends from many people, both related and not, whom I admire has unexpectedly become my own form of ancestral healing. It allows me to assemble my own puzzle pieces, connecting with these people's stories, their passions, and their challenges, as well as reconnecting with some of my own and allowing space for others to join in.

Using the tenets presented for both approaches, we all have our moments when we need to switch to **iiwii.** mode and have the fortitude to say a strong no to the shoulds and yes to ourselves and the quiet voice that says, "Let's rest now, dear one." Alternately, we may find we need to kick into **iiwii?** gear and say yes to a challenge and no to the grating voice that says, "Who are you fooling, anyway? *You* can't do this."

Storytelling, noticing, and sharing these very nuanced yet surprisingly universal **iiwii** moments serve to bring us all together, allowing connection and understanding to emerge, as well as some ideas on how to work with and through these moments. Intentionally creating a community that supports each other during serene times of slowing down and joyous moments of productive activity is an integral part, if not the essence, of what I believe ancestral healing to be. Our community can consist of both those related to us by wiring and those we intentionally and beautifully decide to splice in. We are all the richer when it includes others from different generations, cultures, backgrounds, and experiences. As each of us lands on higher ground, we all do.

REVOLUTIONARY

Through **iiwii?**, we are answering a call to action and doing it in a way that often, if not always, requires a shift in our thinking. Coincidentally, as I was starting this section, I happened to look up at an old bulletin board in my loft and saw a tattered image of a person's head with the words "The first revolution is when you change your mind." I love it, and yet I differ. I think the first revolution is when we *open* our minds, which has to happen before we can then change them. We all have our opinions, perspectives, and criteria for living a "good" life that we have either come up with on our own or unknowingly/subconsciously gotten through others.

I once heard these biased inclinations and filters called "already listenings." It's the notion that we hear what we want to hear, what we are already listening for. For many of us, our codes of moral, professional, and interpersonal conduct are well in place, and we feel have earned the right to keep them there. Some that I've heard floating in my familial and ancestral waterways include:

"If it ain't broke, don't fix it."

"Lead, follow, or get out of the way."

"Pronouns are ridiculous. I'm not going to subject myself to the mental gymnastics to support that inane newfangled idea."

These passed-down ways of thinking, some older, some more recent, could use some unlearning. I am part of the Baby Boomer crew, and our generational DNA around many of these ways of thinking is strong and well-entrenched.

When we hit the flipping point and turned the book upside down to start reading part two, the concept of unlearning was subtly being presented. This is not how we are supposed to read a book. I was thrilled when I found a publisher who not only didn't laugh at the idea but immediately embraced it and figured out a way to do it. Unlearning is central to the **iiwii?** philosophy. We need to clear the decks, shake the Etch A Sketch, and not rest on the laurels of what has always been. Even if what

has always been has been really good, chances are it could use a refresh from time to time.

Going even a bit further, **iiwii?** suggests something splashier than a refresh or touch-up. It is much more dramatic than the slower evolutionary process of **iiwii.**, which often requires patience and letting things gradually work themselves out, embracing the mystery and the uncertainty of the process along the way. The **iiwii?** approach prompts either the changing or the leaving of a situation in order for something very different to emerge. Referred to as a second-order change, it means something that is not incremental but serves to reframe everything as we currently know it.

Along this **iiwii?** line of revolutionary change, there is a Spanish phrase that resonates, which I've always liked: *ya no*. Translated, it means "no longer." There is something that I no longer can accept, and it is time to take action. It's opening our minds to doing something new, designing or approaching something in a completely different way. For some, it could be a "big R" revolutionary effort, like creating something new, a solution to a problem, a system to support a whole new industry around something that had never been done before, like creating my proprietary kit for thorn extractions. Or, I suppose, like aviation.

While **iiwii.** is more of an *experiential discovery*, **iiwii?** tends to fall in the camp of an *intellectual understanding*. We are building our vision after we have asked the appropriate questions to form our vision. It requires new thinking, new insights, and new ways to look at what is. The ability to focus and to intentionally choose are key ingredients, trying one thing and then being completely open to switching gears and even starting over if what we thought would surely work doesn't. Timeframes, checklists, and measurable goals are givens.

For me, it was "I am going to find one thing, even if it is clearing out a gnarly morass of thorns and rats' nests in my backyard." For Hannah, it was summoning up the courage to recite a poem in public or sporting a creative, meaning-filled tattoo in private. It often involves a big yes when we'd prefer to say an emphatic "No, are you kidding me?" With **iiwii?**, keeping Frida cleared out and authoring this book are my acts of saying yes, my small revolution. I have been writing stories and journaling since I

was a young girl but never had the courage or mindset to venture into the world of actual authorship.

In order to pull this off, the notion of understanding and creating a vision for the book was one thing, but figuring out a way to execute it, actually carving out time and space to write it, I realized, meant a completely different approach. Perhaps a retreat to transform an outline into chapters (i.e., to start writing)? I reached my own flipping point and pulled a *ya no*, enough is enough.

I gifted myself with a radical act of rest, a well-earned **iiwii.**/**iiwii?** getaway. It was a time of relaxing and allowing space for some much-needed insight to bubble forth. As referenced earlier, I decided to take a mini sabbatical. I punched out of my everyday life, flew across the country by myself, and hit the beach. In spite of my earlier whining about jellyfish and shark fins, it was rejuvenating and breathtaking; I love the ocean. Shockingly, even more unforgettable and magical than the beach was the Wright brothers memorial I visited just a few miles away in Kitty Hawk. Remember, this was a writer's retreat. I was doing research.

I finally got to experience firsthand all that I had researched and read about regarding these two "crazy boys" my grandmother had talked about since I was little. I got to see the famous stretch of 120 feet that marked the official first flight. I saw the glorified shed that became their home away from home while they were working daily from sunup to sundown to make their obsession (dream) a reality. Witnessing it up close clearly revealed what it looks like to pursue a passion, a calling that we feel to our core we are meant to listen to, hear, and follow. Years ago, I came up with my own definition:

Passion = something we simply can't *not* do.

It was written over every inch of this place. Seeing the now-famous sand dune that they scaled hundreds, if not thousands, of times to test and smash their latest version of a flying machine was especially awe-inspiring. Doing this day in and day out was literally something they couldn't not do. The dune is no longer even sandy. It has lovely green grass covering it with a pristine walkway taking visitors up to the very top so they can see the view and the extraordinary monument built in Wilbur and Orville's honor.

It was no piece of cake, by the way, walking up that steep hill. This coming from someone who hikes in mountain canyons at least once or twice a year. Also, I unwisely wore sandals.

I cannot *imagine* dragging a massive contraption with wings, strings, an engine, propellers, etc. up that tall, steep hill day after day, multiple times a day. I struggled even with a nifty walkway and have no idea how they clambered up when it used to be an unstable, unforgiving sand dune. Just seeing the whole setup spoke volumes about what these nineteenth- and twentieth-century geniuses and their team accomplished.

The most magical moment of that afternoon for me came from something totally unexpected. If I hadn't been by myself, I never would have caught it. Adjacent to one of the fields of this vast and mesmerizing multi-acre Wright Brothers National Memorial and museum, there was another airstrip—this one a modern-day version. It was actually part of a small airpark, placed in beautiful juxtaposition to this site where it literally all began. I had noticed all afternoon that small airplanes were occasionally taking off and landing but had not really paid much attention to it.

As I was about to leave this incredible place, more in awe than ever at what these two brothers had accomplished, I decided to go out one more time to take in my favorite part. It was the short, grassy area where that first successful December 1903 flight took place. I was jotting down some research notes, deep into postulation that perhaps the term *runway* had actually originated from this very spot, where the whole crew had to run alongside the early airplane prototypes, steadying them until they could catch enough momentum and launch into the air. Pleased with myself for connecting this origination-of-the-term-*runway* dot, I closed my small notepad. It was then that I noticed something.

Standing next to one of the rocks with an informational plaque wedged into its side was a young girl, probably around nine or ten years old. I noticed she kept staring with an incredibly intense, fixed gaze at something over in the distance by the edge of the field. Here she was, on this famous spot, and it appeared she was mesmerized by a bunch of trees.

Suddenly, I heard her scream, and I thought something awful had happened. I then realized it wasn't fear; it was a shriek of pure joy. She

shouted to her father, who was close by, reading the same rock, and exclaimed, "Wow! So that's what it looks like to fly! I've never seen an airplane take off before."

Wow. On so many levels. I'm so used to seeing airplanes take off and land. I'm so accustomed to flying in them, being frustrated by them, and being mad they are now charging for every single amenity under the sun that I didn't even notice that *that* was what she was looking at: *an airplane*. How ironic. And I thought it was some strange thing coming out of the small forest of trees.

All I could think about was what we take for granted sometimes. I felt incredibly humbled. I felt even more so when I read, while continuing to do my *Book of iiwii* research, that only 5–6 percent of the entire world population has ever flown in an airplane.[1] Mind blown. Something that so many of us take for granted that so few will ever get to experience. For both me and the young girl, that day truly was a (capital R) Revolutionary experience.

REMOVE THE ROCK

When discussing the shift that took place when the Wright brothers were finally ready to embark on their mission, I noted it was as though they were possessed and obsessed. Probably because I was traipsing around that whole day in my sandals, which rocks kept flying into, I kept getting the image of sharp rocks in shoes that have to be removed: utterly annoying, and yet we cannot ignore them when they get lodged, especially the sharp ones. When dealing with the more transformative changes involved with **iiwii?**, there can often be a precursor of something incredibly irritating, often painful, that we have no choice but to pay attention to and somehow extract from the plan.

It is unlike our **iiwii.** sand in an oyster shell—slightly annoying, but with acceptance and patience, it becomes transformed, transcending into a lovely new creation. This is completely different. These irritations and pain, in my experience, come in a multitude of forms. Basically, they are boulders, large and small, that keep landing in our path while the sharp rocks keep somehow landing in our shoes.

I know I alluded to this before, but, counterintuitively, one of the ways I have come to learn that I am on the right track often is when this barrage of obstacles and ridiculous annoyances starts happening. If I can remember to try to accept them, flex the **iiwii.** muscles, and just let them be, I find they will usually go away. (Not to wish ill on anyone, but perhaps that flat tire, nasty cold, or series of technical mishaps will go find someone else to pester, someone who is perhaps on their own **iiwii?** trailblazing mission.)

This uncomfortable rock in the shoe, obstacle-barrage sensation is a critical point when many get worn down and just want to throw in the towel. Instead of interpreting these barriers as a sign for stopping and going back to the status quo, *now* is the time we need to exercise resistance to that temptation. Like Dory, this is where we just keep swimming. Persistence is paramount.

With **iiwii?**, we embark on a new and emergent quest. With this quest, we know it is now time to take a stand and get past the rocks, debris, and other obstacles through some form of action, even if that action is simply taking a few small steps that maybe don't even make much sense. The first step begets the next. We have our vision, we design the blueprint, and we start to build.

STRINGS ATTACHED

I've always been both attracted to and repelled by the phrase *strings attached*. I think it would be a great title for its own book. For now, however, it will be just a few short paragraphs in the *Book of iiwii.* In the final chapter of **iiwii.**, I talked about loose ends. Now, things get more involved.

With **iiwii?**, there is a call for stepping up to the plate, for showing up for what needs to be done, even if it is just one small effort in our own backyard. With this, there is the notion of responsibility—yes, with strings attached. To pull off these feats, it usually requires a small group of very dedicated people at our side. Or even just *one* person spotting us while we crank up the chainsaw. These sidekicks need to be reliable, committed, and well-informed. We need to know who is doing what, by when, and how. This is an especially tricky string that often seems attached to a

project: if no one is assigned or steps up to do what is needed, then it (most often) doesn't get done.

It is so tempting to say, "Well, isn't it obvious that everyone needs to be doing this, pitching in, doing what needs to be done?" That can actually become a stealthy way for nothing to really get done. Who is responsible for what? My mom was responsible for me and for herself, but if she had stood around trying to explain to me why we needed to blaze one hot trail out of that forest, we'd probably still be there. I can be pretty persuasive (or stubborn) when I want. She knew the only way to get me moving was to get herself moving.

As humans living on and responsible for this planet, we all have strings attached. It is in exercising and acknowledging this responsibility that some of the long-overdue ancestral healing just might start taking place. In her beautifully written book *Wintering*, Katherine May shares:

> You'll find wisdom in your winter, and once it's over, it's your responsibility to pass it on. And in return, it's our responsibility to listen to those who have wintered before us. It's an exchange of gifts in which nobody loses out. This may involve the breaking of a lifelong habit, one passed down carefully through generations, that of looking at other people's misfortunes and feeling certain that they brought them upon themselves in a way that you never would. This isn't just an unkind attitude. It does us harm.[2]

The planet needs vibrancy like never before, and kindness, and compassion. We all need our **iiwii.** "winters" so that we are inspired to slow down and reset. We can then emerge energized to do the work during the seasons that call to us to take action, reminding us that we are all ancestors and descendants of humanity and caretakers of our planet. Our healing is to become part of a whole. Resting in serenity or moving in joy, we are all connected through a beautiful, integrated tangle of strings attached to each other: to forests, bear cubs, mothers, cow skulls, mesquite trees, sand dunes, and airplanes. And jellyfish.

Conclusion

iiwii. and **iiwii?**

*Ask me where I'm from, and I will say a woman, mother, who
breathes sun and moon, light with me. We are the ones who walk
the spine of mother earth, a question on our lips: "How?"
"One step at a time," she says.*

—Kristen A. Sawyer
(American writer, artist, poet, naturalist and teacher)

In exploring **iiwii**, we keep turning concepts on their heads and then
encouraging them to go upright again. I always knew I wanted the book to
be written in an upside-down format, representing the flipping point many
of us reach when realizing we need to make the courageous leap from
what is to something completely different. It takes reorienting, changing
our known way of doing things, and prompts us to open our minds. It's so
annoying at times to have to do things differently.

it is what it is. We grow, or we stagnate.

In the epic movie *Shawshank Redemption*, a discussion between two
inmates beautifully captures this. Andy shares with Red that people either
focus on the business of living or of dying. We grow, or we stagnate. Additionally, Andy adds that the concept of hope is a key ingredient to the
"business of living" option. I agree that hope is a beautiful thing, and in
the case of Andy and Red, it played out with a creative plan involving
hiding wads of money under a tree and ultimately meeting up and retiring

in the small fishing village of Zihuatanejo, Mexico. We have to find what fuels our own spirit.

My hope, my Zihuatanejo, was to get this book completed before my new granddaughter reached high school. I think I may make it. My other hope in writing this was to get to see something I was passionate about—just for me—get done. Creating a deadline and sticking to it were essential. Next came refereeing the competing forces of my right and left brain, which has worked at least for the time being.

When I was in full-blown **iiwii.** mode, feeling my way into the stories, visuals, quotations, and insights that would become part one, it definitely felt more right brain to me. Part two pulled me to take a more quantitative, checklist approach.

I didn't even notice until after I was done that the titles in part two all had the themes for each chapter numbered, written as a formula (Insight #1: Question, Insight #2: Do Something, etc.), while part one didn't. I smiled and just decided to keep it that way. The themes in part one would remain unnumbered and a little softer, looser, with visuals of images and words scattered throughout.

I know I have mentioned certain ahas I've had along the way while both enduring and enjoying the many facets of this **iiwii** journey. Perhaps the biggest aha of all was the realization that so many of our traditional and/or stereotypical ways of viewing life have quite simply become outdated or completely not applicable anymore. As mentioned, the ideas of Eastern versus Western thinking/spirituality/medicine all seem to be blending, swapping, and reconfiguring. Even the time-honored categorization of right-brain versus left-brain dominance and thinking is now being claimed by many to be misguided and not entirely accurate as well.

One of the biggest areas of such blending can be summarized with two colors: pink and blue. Gender stereotyping. I find it interesting to note that early into the research and outlining of **iiwii**, I had started making several references to perspectives being more of a "feminine" nature (the reflective stillness of **iiwii.**) or of a "masculine" leaning (the action bias of **iiwii?**). And yet as I found myself stumbling into this potential pothole, I caught myself.

Fortunately, about that time, I happened to stumble across something else (other than potential potholes, thankfully) that helped me out. Oddly, it was an ancient symbol—the yin-yang circle. I have always felt drawn to it and what I thought it meant: an interplay of some sort between the feminine (yin) and the masculine (yang). I also loved its simple, clean look, so much so that initially I even considered using it on the cover of this book.

In the ever-present reminder that I was writing the book I also needed to read, I tapped back into some of my **iiwii.** learning wisdom. In this case, it was the importance of cultural awareness and context. Don't use the symbol or reference unless homework has been thoroughly done, and even then, think twice. My research yielded more than I possibly could have imagined, including how far off the mark I was in my simplistic under-standing. What I learned was that these two ancient and powerfully com-plementary elements of yin-yang are forces in their own right, so much more than just a compelling symbol. Furthermore, what I realized was that a truly unexpected alignment of yin and yang to my **iiwii.** and **iiwii?** concepts brought in a whole new dimension, both helpful and profound.

Far beyond ideas of simply representing sacred femininity or empow-ered masculinity, the concepts of yin and yang go vastly further. The concept of yin embraces the elements of earth and water, of groundedness and transformation. Going into a cave—Colossal Cave, as an example—is a perfect yin metaphor. The whole notion of going inward, of stillness and darkness (think seed in soil), serves to regenerate and renew us. With yin, there is the soft and connective energy of embracing and noticing, seeing through a lens of both/and, that many possibilities exist. For both yin and **iiwii.**, the hope is that, with the serenity of rest, we become renewed and refreshed.

On the other side of the symbol, the yang concept similarly for me aligns in a beautiful way with **iiwii?**. In asking **is it what it is?** and heeding the pull for a new trajectory, all the characteristics of yang fall into line. Yang ties in with the elements of fire and air, with fire representing passion and creativity. With **iiwii?**, the existence of passion is a prerequi-site to get our new persona (new habits, perspectives, and courage) created

or our new inventions crafted. The Wright brothers literally took to the air, with the lightness, forward motion, and soaring elements of yang energy. This is the energy of the sun and warmth, whereas the energy of yin is said to be of the moon and reflectiveness. For both yang and **iiwii?**, the objective is movement. In taking action, we find joy in the doing and building. We become invigorated.

As a final guest to the **iiwii** party, we have the infinity sign. It is another symbol that seems to follow me around and would not be left out here. While I was tying together loose ends, discovering strings attached and all sorts of other rope and twine connecting in and out, over and over, I realized that the infinity sign was essential to include, and this time it would make the cover. The word comes from the Latin word *infinitas*, meaning "endless," "ongoing," or "unbounded." Interestingly, it's also referred to as *lemniscate* (meaning "ribbon") in algebraic geometry. As a mathematical symbol, it connotes a number that has no end, that is larger than any other number. It means eternal connection, something that can never be broken.

What has become evident to me is that it is the interconnectedness, the movement back and forth of the two **iiwii** concepts just like the ribbon of the infinity sign, that is key to the successful outcome of either idea. We have to do an **iiwii.** to get ourselves rejuvenated with fresh insight to then move into the place of **iiwii?**. The constant work of asking, doing, and building loses its effectiveness if there is not a pause to rest and reorient. Accepting, slowing down, and embracing the unknowns will eventually need to be balanced with some sort of action like blazing new trails, befriending new trees, and/or designing personal mini sabbaticals.

As with yin-yang, with too much of one or the other, things will be off balance. When the back-and-forth flow takes place between **iiwii.** and **iiwii?**, represented by the infinity symbol, serenity from rest, restoration, and subtle insight will be balanced with the joy in activity, accomplishment, and building something meaningful.

Pulling the lens back and reflecting on my *Book of iiwii* journey, it seemed that all along the way, clichés, acronyms, and random ideas would not stop bombarding me: notions of *be* versus *do*, *accept* versus *never settle* (a

tagline for the university in my town as I was writing this), *self-care* versus *other-care*, and more.

I was really tempted to title this book *And Yet*. Every time I would think of something in one way, the inverse or the reverse seemed to then gradually bubble up and reach out to me like the branches of Frida, slightly annoying yet unavoidably compelling at the same time.

What are some of the ways of being and concepts that, as varied cultures and possibly a species, we need to be learning or unlearning? Again, this is so much easier said than done. For so many of us, it has been the water we have been swimming in for so long that it is impossible to see beyond our respective oceans, ponds, lakes, or rivers. Maybe we all need to just hop out of our own ancestral waterways and take to the skies, like Wilbur and Orville, and learn to soar.

Writing this book has been a most unusual process. I don't think I've ever wanted to do anything less in some ways, all the while feeling like I had no choice (a choiceless choice) but to figure out a way, a system, to get it done. And yet at the same time, it has been exhilarating and meaningful beyond words to be able to get these observations, thoughts, and stories on paper.

As I have been giving birth to this book, my daughter (the one who married Frank under Frida) has given birth to an incandescently amazing baby girl named Alia. Every great creation, be it a baby, book, tattoo, or flying machine, comes from one place. This place or source is *passion*.

Writing the *Book of iiwii* is something I couldn't not do. For me, it's been an opportunity to learn new approaches to finding serenity and a sense of vibrant inner well-being during the insanity and the beauty of the times we live in. It's also been an opportunity to rethink, question, and unlearn concepts that (more often than I'd like to admit), I embrace just because I always have.

Whoever you are, even and/or especially if you are my cherished family and friends, I hope you have enjoyed embarking on this journey with me. For some, the route to transformation may be through **it is what it is.**. I see this evolutionary approach—cultivating acceptance, stillness, flow, and mystery—as a twenty-first-century lifesaving skill. For others, it

may be through asking the important and possibly revolutionary question **is it what it is?**. With this, I see inspired doing, collaboration, and emergent system-building with unlearning "the way it's always been" as an essential humanity- and planet-saving skill.

iiwii. or iiwii?

For many of us, it may be both.
For the sake of our planet,
I think it may need to be both.
Godspeed.

—Kathy Lewis Sawyer

"NEVER underestimate a woman with a CHAINSAW"

Suddenly I was on a mission.
Truly, a choiceless choice was being made.

ACKNOWLEDGMENTS

"My heart is a mountain meadow fed by many different streams." These words by author Julia Cameron beautifully capture my experience with the writing of this book. So many different streams of love, patience, laughter, tears, feedback, and heartfelt contributions have all gone into making the *Book of iiwii* happen. Each one of you who has played a part in this truly emergent process knows who you are. My appreciation for your wisdom and support is as boundless as the energy at Kitty Hawk and as deep as the ocean over which I now fly to visit our Firle cousins.

I dedicate *Book of iiwii* to my beloved husband, Chuck, and to my family—immediate and extended, two- and four-legged— without whose support, patience, and existence none of this would have happened. My gratitude truly is beyond words.

iiwii?

ENDNOTES

CHAPTER SIX

1 Eckhart Tolle, *The Power of Now* (Vancouver, Canada: Namaste Publishing, 1997), 68.

2 Anne Lamott, *Bird by Bird: Some Instructions on Writing and Life* (New York: Vintage, 1994), 218.

3 Ailsa Harvey, "Inside a Lighthouse: Discover the Tried-and-Tested Technology Behind These Maritime Navigational Beacons," *How Things Work*, September 1, 2023, https://gb.readly.com/magazines/how-it-works/2023-09-01/.

CHAPTER SEVEN

1 "Millions Owe Their Lives to Mayflower Passenger Who Fell Overboard," *Mayflower 400* (February 2020): https://www.mayflower400uk.org/education/who-were-the-pilgrims/2020/february/john-howland/.

2 Barry Bradford, "'South Pacific' and Racism—Oscar Hammerstein's Moral Cause" (April 23, 2019): https://barrybradford.com/south-pacific-and-racism/.

3 Quoted in Marty Nemko, "From Stress to Genes, Baboons and Hormones: An Interview with Robert Sapolsky," *Psychology Today* (February 4, 2017): https://www.psychologytoday.com/us/blog/how-do-life/201702/stress-genes-baboons-hormones.

4 Malcolm Gladwell, *Talking to Strangers: What We Should Know about the People We Don't Know* (New York: Little, Brown, 2019). Note: I found the stories "Step Out of the Car" (p. 1) and "Case Study: The Boy in the Shower" (p. 107) particularly compelling.

5 Maya Angelou, "Caged Bird," in *Shaker, Why Don't You Sing?* (New York: Penguin Random House, 1983), 16, 17.

6 Charlotte Cabot, "Why Headspace Co-Founder Andy Puddicombe Doesn't Subscribe to the Conventional Notion of Failure," *Thrive Global* (April 18, 2019): https://community.thriveglobal.com/why-headspace-co-founder-any-puddicombe-doesn-t-subscribe-to-the-conventional-notion-of-failure/.

7 Sigal Samuel, "The Surprising Benefits of Contemplating Your Death," *Vox* (August 12, 2020): https://www.vox.com/21363483/mindfulness-of-death-mortality-meditation-nikki-mirghafori.

8 Samuel, "The Surprising Benefits."

9 Bruce H. Lipton, *The Biology of Belief: Unleashing the Power of Consciousness, Matter and Miracles* (Carlsbad, CA: Hay House, 2016), 14, 26.

81

CHAPTER EIGHT

1 See "Dentist Recommends," *Stanford Research into the Impact of Tobacco Advertising* (April 11, 2021): https://tobacco.stanford.edu/cigarette/img0162/.

2 Elmer Bernstein's score for *The Magnificent Seven*, especially its title theme, was among the most popular Western movie music ever written. (The title tune became the "Marlboro Cigarette Theme.")

3 Brian Krans, "Quitting Smoking? Expect Failure before You Succeed," Healthline.com, (July 12, 2016): https://www.healthline.com/health-news/quitting-smoking-expect-failure-before-you-succeed.

4 Jean Mendoza, "What Happened to Etch a Sketch?," Grunge.com (February 28, 2022): https://www.grunge.com/781920/what-happened-to-etch-a-sketch/.

5 Katie Milkman, *How to Change: The Science of Getting from Where You Are to Where You Want to Be* (New York: Penguin, 2021), 26.

6 As quoted in Laura W. Geller, "Katherine Milkman on Why Fresh Starts Matter," *Strategy+Business* (August 8, 2014): https://www.strategy-business.com/article/00266.

7 Fredrickson, *Positivity*, 41.

8 Eckhart Tolle, The Power of Now (Vancouver, Canada: Namaste Publishing, 1997), 68.

9 "Mesquite Trees: Types, Leaves, Flowers, Bark—Identification Guide (with Pictures)," *Leafy Place*, https://leafyplace.com/mesquite-trees/.

10 C. E. Clark, "All about Mesquite or Devil Trees," *Dengarden* (March 30, 2022): https://dengarden.com/landscaping/mesquite-trees-mesquite-bushes-devil-trees-thorns-seedpods.

11 Mary McMahon, "What Are Nurse Trees?," *All Things Nature* (December 29, 2022): https://www.allthingsnature.org/what-are-nurse-trees.html.

12 Carol S. Dweck, *Mindset: The New Psychology of Success* (New York: Ballantine, 2006), 232.

13 J. K. Rowling, "The Fringe Benefits of Failure, and the Importance of Imagination," Harvard University Commencement Address, *Harvard Gazette* (June 5, 2008): https://news.harvard.edu/gazette/story/2008/06/text-of-j-k-rowling-speech/.

14 Mark Galloway, "Mandela: From Prison to President," Documentary, Network First (April 26, 1994): https://www.imdb.com/title/tt6369882/.

CHAPTER NINE

1 David McCullough, *The Wright Brothers*, (New York: Simon & Schuster, 2015), 32.

2 David McCullough, *The Wright Brothers*, (New York: Simon & Schuster, 2015), 33.

3 David McCullough, *The Wright Brothers*, (New York: Simon & Schuster, 2015), 34.

4 Mary Bellis, "Orville's and Wilbur's Thoughts on Flight and Life," *ThoughtCo*, https://www.thoughtco.com/famous-quotes-of-the-wright-brothers-1992679.

5 Fred C. Kelly, "Orville Wright, Letter to His Father and Sister, Kitty Hawk, November 15, 1903," Miracle at Kitty Hawk: Unpublished Letters of the Wright Brothers (Part III), *The Atlantic* (July 1950): https://www.theatlantic.com/magazine/archive/1950/07/miracle-at-kitty-hawk-unpublished-letters-of-the-wright-brothers-part-iii/306539/.

6 William H. Danforth, *I Dare You!* (St. Louis, MO: Ralston-Purina, 1931). As *Scribd* describes, "Considered to be one of the most important self-help books ever written, *I Dare You!* was first published in 1931 [then later in 1942] by William Danforth, the founder of the Ralston-Purina pet food company and the American Youth Foundation. In it, he expounded on his belief that a healthy and productive life depended on keeping four important elements in balance. These elements were physical, mental, social, and religious." See https://www.scribd.com/book/491042453/I-Dare-You.

7 David McCullough, *The Wright Brothers*, (New York: Simon & Schuster, 2015) 9. As a fun and endearing aside, to each other, the trio was known as Ullam: (Wilbur) derived from Jullam, the

German version of William, which it is thought his German maternal grandparents may have called him; Bubbo/Bubs (Orville), which originated from Wilbur's early attempts to pronounce *brother* after Orville was born; and Sterchens (Katharine), which roughly translates into "little sister" in German.

8 Hadley Meares, "Orville and Wilbur: The Brothers Who Changed Aviation," *Biography* (September 9, 2020): https://www.biography.com/inventors/orville-wilbur-wright-brothers-first-flight.

9 As quoted in "Wernher von Braun: Following the Legacy of the Wright Brothers," *Wright Stories*, https://www.wrightstories.com/aviators.html.

10 Phil Scott, "What Were They Thinking? The Wonderful, Unworkable World of Airplane Design in the Years before the Wright Brothers," *Smithsonian* (March 2001): https://www.smithsonianmag.com/air-space-magazine/what-were-they-thinking-1965721/.

11 David McCullough, *The Wright Brothers*, (New York: Simon & Schuster, 2015) 8.

12 David McCullough, *The Wright Brothers*, (New York: Simon & Schuster, 2015) 14.

13 David McCullough, *The Wright Brothers*, (New York: Simon & Schuster, 2015) 8.

14 Rinpoche with Swanson, *Joyful Wisdom*, 40.

15 Tracy Dennis-Tiwary, "In Praise of Anxiety: Using Anxiety to Survive and Thrive," *Wall Street Journal* (May 6, 2022): https://www.wsj.com/articles/in-praise-of-anxiety-11651849496.

16 Tracy Dennis-Tiwary, *Future Tense: Why Anxiety Is Good for You (Even Though It Feels Bad)* (New York: Harper Wave, 2022).

17 Dennis-Tiwary, "In Praise of Anxiety."

18 "Twenty of the Best Wright Brothers Quotes," Bookroo, https://bookroo.com/quotes/wright-brothers.

19 "Twenty of the Best Wright Brothers Quotes."

20 Michael Goodman, "Systems Thinking: What, Why, When, Where, and How," *The Systems Thinker* (2018): https://thesystemsthinker.com/systems-thinking-what-why-when-where-and-how/.

21 Scott, "What Were They Thinking?"

22 Mounted display at Wright Brothers National Memorial (US National Park Service), Kill Devil Hills, North Carolina. Established March 2, 1927. On part of this amazing 431-acre tribute to the Wright brothers, I saw this description on a plaque at the base of the largest dune on the site.

23 Dweck, *Mindset*, 67.

24 St. Benedict, as quoted by Jodi Blazek Gehr, "Always, We Begin Again," *Being Benedictine* (January 4, 2017): https://beingbenedictine.com/2017/01/04/always-we-begin-again/. St. Benedict was an Italian monk, writer, and theologian who died in 547 CE.

25 McCullough, *The Wright Brothers*, 54.

26 Parker Houston, "All Great Thinking Begins with a Growth Mindset: An Illustration from History," *Lead You First* (April 28, 2022): https://leadyoufirst.com/all-great-thinking-begins-with-a-growth-mindset/.

27 John C. Maxwell, *Failing Forward: Turning Mistakes into Stepping Stones for Success* (Nashville, TN: Thomas Nelson, 2007).

28 Meares, "Orville and Wilbur."

29 McCullough, *The Wright Brothers*, 108.

30 McCullough, *The Wright Brothers*, 108.

31 Atul Gawande, *The Checklist Manifesto: How to Get Things Right* (Dallas, TX: Metropolitan Press, 2009).

32 Joi Ito and Jeff Howe, "Emergent Systems Are Changing the Way We Think," Aspen Institute

(January 30, 2017): https://www.aspeninstitute.org/blog-posts/emergent-systems-changing-way-think/.

33 brown, *Emergent Strategy*, 52–53.

CHAPTER TEN

1   Ted Thornhill, "Only FIVE PER CENT of the World's Population Has Ever Been on an Aircraft: 39 Incredible Plane Facts Revealed," *Daily Mail* (February 3, 2017): https://www.dailymail.co.uk/travel/travel_news/article-4185292/The-amazing-plane-facts-ever.html#.

2   Katherine May, *Wintering* (New York: Riverhead, 2020), 122.

BIBLIOGRAPHY

Adams, Douglas. *The Hitchhiker's Guide to the Galaxy*. Great Britain: Pan Books, Ltd., 1979.

Angelou, Maya. "Caged Bird." *Shaker, Why Don't You Sing?* New York, NY: Random House, 1983.

Associated Press. "John B. Gage Led Missouri Reform." *New York Times* (January 16, 1970): https://www.nytimes.com/1970/01/16/archives/john-b-gage-led-missouri-reform-kansas-city-mayor-after-pendergasts.html.

Bailey, Elisabeth Tova. *The Sound of a Wild Snail Eating*. Chapel Hill, NC: Algonquin, 2010.

Beck, Martha. *Finding Your Way in a Wild New World*. New York: Free Press, 2012.

———. *The Joy Diet*. New York: Crown, 2003.

Bisko, Andrea. "The Lost Generation Writers in the 1920s." Study.com (September 13, 2021): https://study.com/learn/lesson/the-lost-generation-expatriate-writers-of-the-20th-century.html.

Bradford, Barry. "'South Pacific' and Racism—Oscar Hammerstein's Moral Cause." Barry Bradford (April 23, 2019): https://barrybradford.com/south-pacific-and-racism/.

brown, adrienne maree. *Emergent Strategy: Shaping Change, Changing Worlds*. Chico, CA: AK Press, 2017.

Bryant, Austin. "All about Boro—The Story of Japanese Patchwork—Japanese Upcycle: The Art of Boro." *Heddel* (August 31, 2015): https://www.heddels.com/2015/08/all-about-boro-story-japanese-patchwork/.

Burkeman, Oliver. *Four Thousand Weeks: Time Management for Mortals*. New York: Farrar, Straus and Giroux, 2021.

Cabot, Charlotte. "Why Headspace Co-Founder Andy Puddicombe Does Not Subscribe to the Conventional Notion of Failure." *Thrive Global* (April 18, 2019): https://community.thriveglobal.com/why-headspace-co-founder-any-puddicombe-doesn-t-subscribe-to-the-conventional-notion-of-failure/.

Coleman, Daniel. "John B. Gage." The Pendergast Years, Kansas City Public Library. https://pendergastkc.org/article/biography/john-b-gage.

Cummings, Michael K., and Robert N. Proctor. "The Changing Public Image of Smoking in the United States: 1964–2014." National Library of Medicine (January 23, 2014): https://www.ncbi.nlm.nih.gov/pmc/articles/PMC3894634/.

Danforth, William H. *I Dare You!* St. Louis, MO: Ralston Purina, 1931.

Davis, Wade. *Wayfinders: Why Ancient Wisdom Matters in the Modern World*. Toronto: House of Anansi, 2009.

Dennis-Tiwary, Tracy. *Future Tense: Why Anxiety Is Good for You (Even Though It Feels Bad)*. New York: Harper Wave, 2022.

———. "In Praise of Anxiety: Using Anxiety to Survive and Thrive." *Wall Street Journal*, May 6, 2022. https://www.wsj.com/articles/in-praise-of-anxiety-11651849496.

Doubek, Alli. "You Wouldn't Worry What Other People Think of You if You Knew How Seldom They Do." Dancing through the Rain (February 14, 2017): https://dancingthroughtherain.com/you-wouldnt-worry-what-other-people-think-if-you-knew-how-seldom-they-do/.

Doyle, Glennon. *Untamed*. New York: Dial, 2022.

Dweck, Carol S. *Growth Mindset: The New Psychology of Success*. New York: Ballantine, 2006.

Economy, Peter. "The Stupidity of 'It Is What It Is . . .'" *Inc.* (November 12, 2015): https://www.inc.com/peter-economy/the-stupidity-of-it-is-what-it-is.html.

Einstein, Albert. *Living Philosophies*. New York: Simon & Schuster, 1931.

Fredrickson, Barbara L. *Positivity: Discover the Upward Spiral That Will Change Your Life*. New York: Harmony, 2009.

Gawande, Atul. *The Checklist Manifesto: How to Get Things Right*. Dallas, TX: Metropolitan Press, 2009.

Geller, Laura. "Katherine Milkman on Why Fresh Starts Matter." *Strategy+Business* (August 8, 2014): https://www.strategy-business.com/article/00266.

Gladwell, Malcolm. *Talking to Strangers: What We Should Know about the People We Don't Know*. New York: Little, Brown, 2019.

Gober, Mark. *An End to Upside Down Thinking: Dispelling the Myth That the Brain*

Produces Consciousness, and the Implications for Everyday Life. Cardiff-by-the-Sea, CA: Waterside, 2018.

Goodman, Michael. "Systems Thinking: What, Why, When, Where, and How." *The Systems Thinker*, (2018): https://thesystemsthinker.com/systems-thinking-what-why-when-where-and-how/.

Grysolle, Charlotte. "5 Japanese Life Philosophies Worth Knowing." (May 6, 2022): https://www.charlottegrysolle.com/5-japanese-life-philosophies-worth-knowing/.

Hargrove, Faye. *Better Choices: When We Know Better, We Do Better*. Aiken, SC: Stewart and Associates, 2009.

Harvey, Ailsa. "Inside a Lighthouse: Discover the Tried-and-Tested Technology Behind These Maritime Navigational Beacons." *How Things Work*, September 1, 2023. https://gb.readly.com/magazines/how-it-works/2023-09-01/.

Hersey, Tricia. *Rest Is Resistance: A Manifesto*. New York: Little, Brown Spark, 2022.

Houston, Parker. "All Great Thinking Begins with a Growth Mindset: An Illustration from History." *Lead You First* (April 28, 2022): https://leadyoufirst.com/all-great-thinking-begins-with-a-growth-mindset/.

Katie, Byron. *Loving What Is: Four Questions That Can Change Your Life*. New York: Harmony, 2002.

Katie, Byron, and Stephen Mitchell. *A Thousand Names for Joy: Living in Harmony with the Way Things Are*. New York: Harmony, 2007.

Kimball, Donny. "Uketamo (I Accept)—Training with the Dewa Sanzan Yamabushi." *A Different Side of Japan* (November 15, 2019): https://donnykimball.com/yamabushi-dewa-sanzan-f724a057d7a4.

Lamott, Anne. *Bird by Bird: Some Instructions on Writing and Life*. New York: Vintage, 1994.

Lipton, Bruce H. *The Biology of Belief: Unleashing the Power of Consciousness, Matter and Miracles*. Carlsbad, California: Hay House, 2016.

Maxwell, John C. *Failing Forward: Turning Mistakes into Stepping Stones for Success*. Nashville, TN: Thomas Nelson, 2007.

May, Katherine. *Wintering: The Power of Rest and Retreat in Difficult Times*. New York: Riverhead, 2020.

McArthur, Shirin. "Considering Pronouns in a Changing Culture." (April 29,

2024): https://shirinmcarthur.com/2024/04/29/considering-pronouns-in-a-changing-culture/.

McCollam, Douglas. "It Is What It Is . . . But What Is It?" *Slate* (February 15, 2006): https://slate.com/culture/2008/02/it-is-what-it-is-a-sports-cliche-for-our-times.html.

McCullough, David. *The Wright Brothers*. New York: Simon & Schuster, 2015.

McGonigal, Kelly. *The Will Power Instinct: How Self-Control Works, Why It Matters, and What You Can Do to Get More of It*. New York: Penguin, 2012.

McMahon, Mary. "What Are Nurse Trees?" *All Things Nature* (December 29, 2022): https://www.allthingsnature.org/what-are-nurse-trees.html.

Meares, Hadley. "Orville and Wilbur: The Brothers Who Changed Aviation." *Biography* (September 9, 2020): https://www.biography.com/inventors/orville-wilbur-wright-brothers-first-flight.

Meeks, Catherine. *Night Is Long but Light Comes in the Morning: Meditations for Racial Healing*. Harrisburg, PA: Morehouse, 2022.

Mendoza, Jean. "What Happened to Etch A Sketch?" *Grunge* (February 28, 2022): https://www.grunge.com/781920/what-happened-to-etch-a-sketch/.

Mendoza, Katya. "Creosote Bush Heals from the Inside Out." *Foothills News* (July 27, 2022): 4.

Milkman, Katie. *How to Change: The Science of Getting from Where You Are to Where You Want to Be*. New York: Penguin, 2021.

"Millions Owe Their Lives to Mayflower Passenger Who Fell Overboard." *Mayflower 400* (February 2020): https://www.mayflower400uk.org/education/who-were-the-pilgrims/2020/february/john-howland/.

Moodley, Nisha. "Procrastination vs. Percolation (and How to Tell the Difference)." Nisha Moodley (August 24, 2012): https://nishamoodley.com/procrastination-vs-percolation/.

Moran, Victoria. *Creating a Charmed Life*. New York: Harper Collins, 1999.

O'Donohue, John. *Eternal Echoes: Celtic Reflections on Our Yearning to Belong*. New York: HarperCollins, 1998.

Phillips, Adam. *Missing Out: In Praise of the Unlived Life*. London: Picador, 2013.

Pink, Daniel. *The Power of Regret: How Looking Backward Moves Us Forward*. New York: Penguin, 2022.

Pressfield, Stephen. *Do the Work! Overcome Resistance and Get Out of Your Own Way.* North Egremont, MA: Black Irish Entertainment, 2011.

———. *The War of Art: Break Through the Blocks and Win Your Inner Creative Battles.* New York: Warner, 2002.

Rector, Barbara. *Adventures in Awareness: Learning with the Help of Horses.* Bloomington, IN: AuthorHouse, 2005.

Richardson, James. "Vectors 3.0: Even More Aphorisms and Ten-Second Essays." *Gwern* (November 28, 2018): https://www.gwern.net/docs/philosophy/2010-richardson-bythenumbers-vectors30.

Rinpoche, Yongey Mingyur, with Eric Swanson. *Joyful Wisdom: Embracing Change and Finding Freedom.* New York: Three Rivers, 2009.

Rodriguez, Lisa. "80 Years Post-Pendergast, Kansas City Mayoral Hopefuls Wonder If Local Control of Police Is Worth It." *NPR/KCUR Politics Elections and Government*, March 29, 2019. https://www.kcur.org/politics-elections-and-government/2019-03-29/80-years-post-pendergast-kansas-city-mayoral-hopefuls-wonder-if-local-control-of-police-is-worth-it.

Rumi, Jelaluddin. "Out beyond Ideas of Wrongdoing and Rightdoing." In *The Essential Rumi.* Translated by Coleman Barks with John Moyne. New York: HarperCollins, 1995. https://poetrysociety.org/poetry-in-motion/out-beyond-ideas-of-wrongdoing-and-rightdoing.

Safire, William. "It Is What It Is: Using Tautophrases to Duck and Deflect." *Taipei Times* (March 5, 2006): https://www.taipeitimes.com/News/editorials/archives/2006/03/05/2003295843.

Santiago, Josie. "How Somatics Can Help Us Get Unstuck." (June 15, 2022): https://www.akiliwell.com/post/how-somatics-can-help-us-get-unstuck/.

Sapolsky, Robert M. *Why Zebras Don't Get Ulcers: A Guide to Stress, Stress-Related Diseases, and Coping.* New York: St. Martin's, 2004.

Scott, Phil. "What Were They Thinking? The Wonderful, Unworkable World of Airplane Design in the Years Before the Wright Brothers." *Smithsonian* (March 2001): https://www.smithsonianmag.com/air-space-magazine/what-were-they-thinking-1965721/.

Simpson, Helen. "The Outsider: Why Katherine Mansfield Still Divides Opinion 100 Years after Her Death." *The Guardian* (January 7, 2023): https://www.theguardian.com/books/2023/jan/07/the-outsider-why-katherine-mansfield-divided-opinion.

Sharma, Rhaki Safta. "Limited Beliefs That Block Your Path to Achieve Goals

and Happiness." LinkedIn (August 5, 2015): https://www.linkedin.com/pulse/limited-beliefs-bloco-your-path-achieve-goals-rakhi-softa-sharma/.

Smith, Andy. "First Order and Second Order Change: Understanding the Difference." Coaching Leaders (June 28, 2018): https://coachingleaders.co.uk/first-order-change/.

Smith, Scott. "Psychology: A Sense of Mystery May Be the Spice of Life." *Capital Gazette* (February 6, 2014): https://www.capitalgazette.com/cg2-arc-140206cl-smith-20140206-story.html.

Tlievna, Ouwtre. *The Simple Essence of Life*. Crested Butte, CO: Self-Published, 2019.

Tolle, Eckhart. *A New Earth: Awakening to Your Life's Purpose*. New York: Penguin/Plume, 2005.

———. *The Power of Now: A Guide to Spiritual Enlightenment*. Novato, CA: New World Library, 1999.

Twist, Lynne. *The Soul of Money*. New York: W. W. Norton, 2017.

Walther, Anne. "What Is Wabi Sabi? The Elusive Beauty of Imperfection." *Japan Objects* (January 8, 2021): https://japanobjects.com/features/wabi-sabi.

Wood, Peter. *Liminal Space*, undated handout.